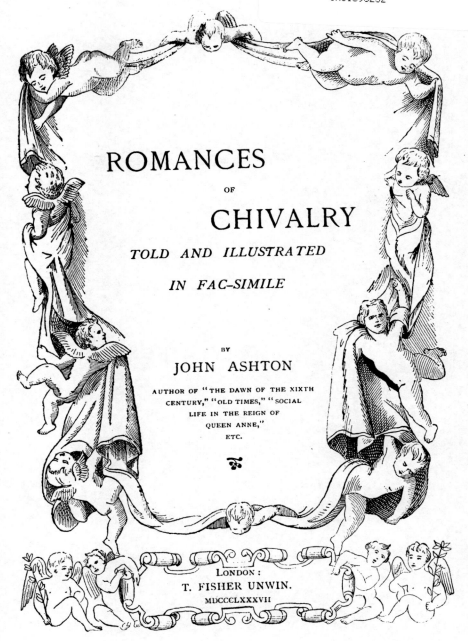

ROMANCES

OF

CHIVALRY

TOLD AND ILLUSTRATED

IN FAC-SIMILE

BY

JOHN ASHTON

AUTHOR OF "THE DAWN OF THE XIXTH
CENTURY," "OLD TIMES," "SOCIAL
LIFE IN THE REIGN OF
QUEEN ANNE,"
ETC.

LONDON:
T. FISHER UNWIN.
MDCCCLXXXVII

THE MYSTERY OF MELUSINE DISCOVERED. [*Frontispiece.*

PREFACE.

TO the general reader the Romances of Chivalry are very little known, some of them not at all ; and the reason of this is, that no efforts have been made to popularize them. Originating, as they did, with the professional story-tellers of Norman times, they were, first of all, metrical histories of the deeds of heroes, like those which the Minstrel Taillefer sung at the Battle of Hastings, when he went before William, chanting of Charlemagne and Roland. Soon these were garnished with tales of love, and, after a time, imagination was called into play, and the Romance was written. They were *the Novels* of the thirteenth to the seventeenth centuries, and must ever be thought of in that light ; they were highly sensational, and full of incident, never prolix, or with long-winded speeches, till they were on the wane, at the end of the sixteenth and beginning of the seventeenth centuries ; and many of them have survived to our days in a condensed form, as chap-books, or books for children—a fact which sufficiently shows the hold they had upon the people.

Some, nay most of them, have been edited and reprinted for the learned societies; but then only the oldest, or rarest MSS., or printed copies, have been thus treated, and they have seldom travelled far from the bookshelves of the subscribers to these societies. And the reason is not far to seek. The language in which they are written is far too archaic for the ordinary reader, and requires a special antiquarian education. The language of the fourteenth and fifteenth centuries is totally different from the English of to-day, and no ordinary person would care about sitting down to read a book which would be unintelligible to him, were he not to refer to a glossary at every line.

Weber, Ritson, and Thoms, did something to bring them into notice, and there is the best book of all on the subject in Bohn's Antiquarian Library; but its usefulness is marred by that awful word "antiquarian." People will not believe that anything can be amusing if under that heading—it must be dry as dust. The popularity of our archæological societies has somewhat dispelled this notion, but the prejudice remains generally.

Is there any reason why they should not be made as attractive as other stories? People will read the Northern Sagas, or North American Indian legends, and tales of wonder; fairy and folk-lore tales are eagerly perused;

whilst the Oriental Romances of the Thousand and One Nights are devoured, not only by the young, but by children of a larger growth. These Romances of Chivalry deal in no greater marvels than are contained in the foregoing examples, and they do give us a wonderful insight into the manners and customs of our own country, centuries ago.

Another reason why these Romances have not been so popular as they might have been is, that they have never been illustrated ; there has never been an attempt to reproduce the contemporary engravings, which are so deliciously quaint, and which throw so much light on the manners and costumes of the period. Many of these wood blocks are far older than the date of the books which they adorn, as may be seen by the broken edges and worm-holes, and have probably illustrated some previous edition now lost to us. To render these Romances more interesting to the general reader, I have facsimiled the engravings, and, as they are my own work, I can guarantee their fidelity.

In making this selection, I have carefully avoided those relating to Charlemagne, believing that the Carlovingian Romances ought to be made into a series of their own ; and I have not touched on the Arthurian legends, which might well make another ; but I have taken those which were thoroughly independent, each of which could stand on its own merits, without reference to another.

PREFACE.

The advanced student may possibly grumble at the number of foot-notes I have appended, in order to elucidate the text, but my object has been, that every one, of average intelligence, who reads the book, may thoroughly understand it, and that without constantly referring to a glossary, which, however, will be found at the end.

JOHN ASHTON.

CONTENTS.

ILLUSTRATIONS.

ROMANCES OF CHIVALRY.

Melusine.

THIS Romance, separated from the other stories which are interwoven with it, is one of the prettiest, and daintiest, of the fanciful tales of the so-called middle ages. It is the story of the fabled rise of the celebrated French family of Lusignan in Poitiers— Sovereign Counts of Forez, or Forest, which furnished kings to Jerusalem and Cyprus.[1]

There are those, however, who hardly look upon the Fairy Melusine as supernatural, but contend that she was a very living and corporal being, named Mélisende,

---

[1] " A Royal Claimant has just disappeared, in the person of a Russian officer, named Lusignan, who held himself entitled to the crown of Cyprus. His death does not, however, remove all danger of our right to rule the island being some day contested, for he has left a son, the solitary attendant at his funeral, who claims not only to be King of Cyprus, but of Jerusalem and Armenia. The Sultan may have some trouble, therefore, as well as ourselves."
—*Globe*, July 10, 1884.

widow of a king of Jerusalem, who married a Geoffrey
de Lusignan ; but there seems to be no foundation for
this report, and, to believe it, would be to render devoid
of all interest the charming *fabliau* of Jean d'Arras,
which was written by him at the command of the Duc
de Berri, who was brother to Charles V. of France. His
sister, the Duchesse de Bar, was probably tired of the
sameness of château life, and the Duc, in order to amuse
her, ordered his secretary to write the story of Melusine
for her delectation.

And right well did he acquit himself of his commission, for the story, *pur et simple*, is simply and most
pathetically told.   The text which I follow, and which
has never been printed, is an English translation of the
Romance of Jean d'Arras, a MS. of the 15th century,
luckily preserved in the British Museum (Royal 18, B. II.),
and it commences thus: "In the begynnyng of all
works / men oughten first of alle to call (on) the name
of the Creator of all creatures / which is very and trew
maister of alle thinges made or to be made that oughten
somwhat to entende to perfection of wele.   Therefore
att the begynnynge of this present historye / though
that I ne be not worthy for to requyre hym / beseche
ryght devoutly, his right highe and worthy mageste
that this present history he wyl helpe me to bring unto
a good ende / and to ful doo it att (to) hys glorye and
praysyng.   And to the plaisure of my right high mighte

THE EARL OF POITIERS' FEAST. [*See p.* 13.

and doubtid [1] lord Johan, sone to the Kyng of ffraunce,
Dñs of Berry and of Auvergne. The whiche hystory
I have bygõne after the veray and true cyronykles whiche
I have had of hy and of the Erle of Salesbury in
England, and many other bokes that I have sought
& ordredde for to accomplysshe hit. And by cause
that his noble suster Marye doughter to the Kyng
Johñ of ffraunce, duchesse of Bar had requyred my said
lord for to have the said historye, the whiche in favour
of her hath doon as moche to his power as he might
to serche the very trouth & true historye / and hath
cõmanded me to do drawe alle alonge thistory whiche
herafter foloweth / . And I as of herte dyligent of my
poure witt & connying (write) as nygh as I can the
pure trouth of hys gracyõs cõmandement. Wherfore
I humbly & devoutly beseche & pray to my Creatour
that my said lord will take it in gr(a)ce / and also all
them that shall rede or here it / that they wil pardonne
me yf I have said enythinge that ben not to theire good
gr(a)ce. Whiche this present hystorye I byganne the
Wensday saynt Clementis day in Winter the yer of
o[r] Lord, m.ccc.lxxxvii. beseching alle them that shall
rede or here it redde that they wil pardonne me my
fawte if their be eny, ffor certaynly I have composed yt
the moost justly that I conde or have mowe after the
cronykles whiche I suppose certaynly to be trew."

[1] Doughty, brave, valiant.

Here, then, we get undoubted evidence both as to the author and the date of its writing. It must have been very popular on the Continent, for a copy printed in French, and printed at Geneva in 1478, is in existence; whilst at the British Museum we possess some very early ones.

In German.	Strasburg.	1478 ? fol.
,,	,,	1480 ? ,,
,,	Augsburg.	1538 ,,
In Spanish.	Tholosa.	1489 4°
,,	Sevilla.	1526 fol.

From that published at Tholosa I have copied the illustrations which I have used, and believe them to be of French work. They are in draughtsmanship and expression almost in advance of their time, and, certainly, are the best woodcuts of any Romance we possess.

Singularly enough, although so well known, and so early printed on the Continent, it does not seem to have been set up in type in this country, there being no record of its ever having engaged the attention of any of our early printers. That it was known in MS. is evidenced from the beautiful copy whence I draw my text, whenever quoted, but the only version that has been printed, was published by the Early English Text Society in 1866: "The Romans of Partenay or of Lusignen : otherwise known as the tale of Melusine : Translated from the French of La Coudrette (about 1500–1520 A.D.) Edited from a unique manuscript in

RAYMONDIN IS LEFT WITH HIS UNCLE. [*See p.* 13

the library of Trinity College, Cambridge, with an Introduction, Notes, and Glossarial Index, by the Rev. Walter W. Skeat, M.A., &c."

This, to the scholar, is a charming book; but it is " caviar to the general." It is in verse, and the language is very archaic; besides which, being a transcript of the whole MS., the stories of Melusine, King Helmas, Geoffry of the Great Tooth, and his brothers, the Lady of the Sparrow-hawk, and Palestine's Treasure, are, as in all the versions of Melusine, very involved. Add to this that it was published by a learned Society, which, although doing a wonderfully good work in behalf of English literature, is not as well known as it deserves to be by the general public, and, rightly following out its *raison d'être*, published it for the benefit of its members and the scholarly public, without reference to the great mass of readers. That it has not been more popular, is somewhat astonishing, seeing that it has been translated from the French into German, Spanish, Danish, and Russ—probably into other languages.

At first sight it would seem that this Romance was indebted to England for its very inception, but Jean d'Arras, who says he tells the truth as far as he possibly can, says, " Hystory recounteth to us that there was som tyme in the Brut [1] Brytayn a noble man whiche

---

[1] The legend runs that Brute, a descendant of Æneas, after the siege of Troy, came over to England and founded London, then called Troy novant, or Tre nevant; but in this Romance, Brittany is evidently meant.

fell at debate with the nevew of the King of Bretons,
and in dede he durst therfore no more dwelle within
the land, but toke with hym al his fynance & goods and
went out of the land by the high mountaynes.   And
as telleth thistorye he founde on a day nighe by a
fontayn a fayre lady to whom he told al his ffortune &
adventure/ so that fynally they enamoured eche other,
and the lady shewed to hym grett love & dede unto
hym moch comfort, and he began within her land that
was wast & deserte for to bylde & make fayre tounes
and strong castels. and was the land within short tyme
peupled raisonably/ and they dide calle the land forestz
by cause that they founde it full of grett wods and
thikk bushes.   And yet at this day it is called fforestz.
It haped that this Knight and this lady fel at debate
togedre.   I ne wot not goodly how ne wherfore / but
that right sodaynly departed the lady fro the Knight
wherfore he was woful & hevy. and notwythstandinge
he grew & increased in worth(y)n(es)s and in prosperite.
The noble men thanne of this land / seeyng that they
were without a lady purveyed hym of oon to hys wyf
a moche gentil & fayre woman suster to the Erle of
Poiters which regned at that tyme, & he begat on her
many children males. among the whiche was oon that
is to wete the iij^de borne which was named Raymondyn
and was fayre goodly & gracyous, moche subtyl & wyty
in all thinges.   And that same tyme the said Raymondin
might be xiiij yere of age."

THE EARL DISCOURSES OF ASTRONOMY. [*See p.* 14.

His uncle, the Earl of Poitiers, had but one son, Bertrand, and, when he was to be dubbed knight, the Earl made a great feast; he invited the Earl of Forest, who was not rich for his position, and, moreover, had many sons, to feast with him. The invitation was accepted, and he took with him three of his boys. It was a great feast, and many a knight was there dubbed, including the eldest son of the Earl of Forest, "ffor he jousted moche wel & fayre." Seven mortal days did this feast continue, and when it came to an end, and the guests were departing, the Earl of Poitiers begged his brother-in-law to leave Raymondin with him, promising that he would provide for his future life. The Earl of Forest consented, and Raymondin was accordingly left with his uncle; and his father, with his two brothers, went home.

The Earl of Poitiers, whose name was Emery, was learned above his peers; " he conde [1] many a science, and specially he was parfytte in the science of Astronomy ;" but also, like every knight and country gentleman, he dearly loved his hound and hawk, of both of which he had many. One day a forester brought word that in the forest of Colombiers "was the moost mervayllous wild bore that had be sene of long tyme byfore, and that at hym shuld be the best & fayrest dysport that eny gentylman shuld ever have."

[1] Knew.

So the Earl, "with grette foyson¹ of barons and knightes," set out to chase this prodigy, Raymondin riding with him as his esquire, and they duly found the wild boar, which "was fel and proude, & devoured & kyld many houndes, and toke his cours thrugh the fforest, ffor he was strongly chaffed,² and they byganne for to folowe hym waloping³ a good paas." But in spite of all their "waloping" the boar took such a line of country that none of the field, save the Earl and Raymondin, cared about following him. Once Raymondin brought the boar to bay and attacked him, but the boar charged, and, sad to say about a hero of romance, knocked Raymondin backwards and then fled. Of course Raymondin remounted and followed him, and the Earl, fearful that the young man might come to grief, spurred after him, and, to his great joy, caught him up.

By this time their horses were somewhat tired, and they rested under a tree until nightfall, when the Earl immediately mounted his hobby of astronomy, and discoursed most learnedly on that science to his nephew, until he noticed such astral conjunctions that he began to weep full sorely; and, on Raymondin questioning him, he told him that there would happen to them a great adventure, and that he foresaw by the stars that, if a subject should slay his lord, he should become the

¹ Company.   ² Very angry.   ³ Galloping.

RAYMONDIN BY MISCHANCE KILLS HIS UNCLE. [*See p.* 17.

most powerful nobleman in the land, and from him should spring such a noble lineage that it should be in memory and remembrance until the end of the world. He further went on to say that he, Earl Emery, was now old, and he so loved Raymondin that he hoped the prognostications of the heavens might be fulfilled in their proper persons.

There were more tears on the part of the Earl and deprecatory protests from Raymondin, when they heard a fearful noise, which they found proceeded from a wonderfully great and horrible boar that was coming straight towards them. Raymondin wished the Earl to climb some tree, but the old nobleman would not forsake his young kinsman, the consequence of which was that the boar left Raymondin and charged the Earl suddenly; who, seeing the enraged animal approach, dropped his sword, and, taking a short spear and running towards the boar, *broched*, or spitted, the brute through the breast, although the shock brought him to his knees. Raymondin at this time came up, and, finding the boar lying on his back, smote him such a blow that his sword broke, and, part of the blade springing backward, pierced the Earl's breast and killed him. The unconscious Raymondin, vexed at the snapping of his sword blade, "toke the spere, and so strongly broched it thrughe the bore that he slew hym."

Then, and not till then, he saw the cruel mishap that

had befallen his uncle. "He went, and wold have had hym to stand upon his feet, but it was for nought, he thenne pulled out of hys brest the piece of the swerde and knew that it was hys dede. Moche mervayllously thanne byganne Raymondin to sighe & to complayne, & wept and lamented piteously, saying in this maner, Ha, ha, false fortune, how moche art thow perverse and evyll that hath doon [1] to be slayn by me hym that loved me so moche, and that had doon to me so moche good. Ha, God Fader Almighty, where shal now be the lande where this harde [2] and false synner shal now abyde, ffor in certayn all they that shall here spek of this grett mysdede shall juge me, and with good right, to dey [3] of a shamfull deth, ffor a more false ne more evyl treson dide never no sinnes. Ha, erthe, cleve [4] and open the, & devoure thou me fourthwith and lete me fall with the moost obscure & derke angel within helle y^t sometime [5] was the fayrest of all other in heven, ffor wel I have deserved it."

For a long time Raymondin thus mourned, calling to mind the Earl's astronomical prediction, how that, if a subject should then slay his lord, he should arrive to high estate, and establish a famous line of descendants. In this, however, he could find no comfort, but, bewailing his sad fate, he only thought of fleeing from the possible consequences of his mishap, and going to some land

[1] Caused.   [2] Hardy.   [3] Die.   [4] Cleave or rend asunder.   [5] That formerly..

RAYMONDIN'S FIRST MEETING WITH MELUSINE. [See p. 21.

where he might do penance for his unconscious sin.
So he knelt down and fondly kissed his dead uncle,
"and soone after that he had kyssed hym, he layd hys
foot in the sterop and leped upon hys hors, and departed,
holding his way through the myddel of the fforest moche
dyscomforted, & rode apas,[1] unknowing the way, ne[2]
whether he went, by only by hap & att aventure. And
made such a sorrow that there was no personne in the
worlde that could think ne say the Vth part of hys
doulour."

"Raymondin was thus pensefull[3] and hevy of herte of
the myshap that was come to hym, that he ne wyst
where he was, ne whither he went, ne in no manere he
ledd hys hors, but hys hors ledd hym where that he wold,
ffor Raymondin touched not the brydell, and herd ne
saw nought, so sore was hys wit troubled."

It was now midnight and bright moonlight, and, in
his abstracted state, he rode along until he came to a fairy
fountain, called the ".fontayne of Soyf," or "Thirsty
Gladness," beautifully situated, in a magnificent country—
and, by this fountain, three fair damsels were disporting,
no others than Melusine and her two sisters, Melior and
Palestine—and of these three, Melusine was evidently the
chief.

Raymondin saw them not, but his horse did, and fled
from them in a fright.

---

[1] Apace—quickly.   [2] Nor.   [3] Pensive—full of thought.

Then Melusine addressed her sisters, and remarked upon the incivility of the rider, who never even made obeisance, or saluted them, as was only ordinary in the days of chivalry. " By my feyth, he that rode now and passed before us semyth to be a moche gentylman, and nevertheles he maketh of it no semblance, but he sheweth the semblaunt [1] of a vylayne or kerle [2] that hath passed so before ladyes without to have salewed [3] them. I goo to make hym spek, ffor he semeth to be a sleep."

So saying, she left her sisters, and went after Raymondin, and, having caught his horse by the bridle, she made him stand still, and began to upbraid the esquire for his uncouth behaviour, but he heard her not, nor answered her. " And she as angry and wroth, sayd ones agen to hym, And how, sire musarde,[4] are ye so dyspytoned [5] that ye dayne [6] not answere to me. And yet he answered nere [7] a word. By my feyth [8] sayd she within herselfe, I byleve non other but that this yong man slepeth upon his hors, or ellis he is eythir dombe or def." So she pulled his hand forcibly, and Raymondin, waking up with a start, all astonished, drew his sword impulsively, and laid about him, thinking that it was some of the Earl's train come to arrest him; but a moment or two brought him to his senses, especially when he heard, amidst

---

[1] Resemblance   [2] A villein or ceorl—a labourer or slave.
[3] Saluted.   [4] Dreamer.   [5] Dispositioned.
[6] Deign.   [7] Never.   [8] Faith.

RAYMONDIN TAKES LEAVE OF MELUSINE. [See p. 29.

rippling laughter, "Sire vassal, with whom will you begynne the bataille: your enemys ben not here, and knowe you fayre sire that I am of your party or side."

Raymondin was struck, as he could not fail to be, with the exquisite beauty of the lady, got off his horse, and knelt before her, after the fashion of his time. He apologised for his involuntary abstraction, and pleaded that he was full of thought—of something which lay heavy on his heart, and of which he prayed to God to relieve him. The fair damsel at once changed her tone of banter to one of seriousness, and put a trial question to him, as to whither he was going. He replied that he knew not—he had lost his way. She, then, seeing he would not tell his secret, sprung her mine upon him. Calling him by name, she told him he should hide nothing from her, for she knew all about him.

Raymondin was utterly astonished at thus hearing himself named by the fair stranger, so that he could not answer her, and she, pursuing the advantage she had gained, told him that, after God, she was the best counsellor he could have; and, to prove her intimate knowledge of his affairs, she told him how that he had slain his lord by mishap, and even related the conversation they had had together on astronomy, promising, if he would but obey her counsels, he should come to no harm, but be the greatest man that had ever been, of his race, as well as the largest landed proprietor.

Raymondin saw that this beautiful being was possessed of almost supernatural powers, but, before he promised he would obey her advice, he prudently inserted a clause, "and it be that a cristen man may or ought to doo with honour." The lady replied after her manner, *Ca va sans dire*, and then established as the first preliminary, that he should promise to make her his wife. This Raymondin at once agreed to. But Melusine had another condition contingent upon this, and, as the story hinges mainly upon this, it is but fit that it should be given in the very words of the MS. "Ye must promysse to me, Raymondyn, upon all the sacrements & other that a man very Catholique & of good faith may do and swere, that never while I shall be in your company, ye shal not peyne ne force yourselfe for to see me on the Saturday, nor by no manere ye shall not enquyre that day of me ne the place where I shall be. And whan she had thus said to Raymondin, he yet ageyn said to her in this manere, On the parel of my sowle I swere to you, that never on y^t day I ne shal doo nothing that may hyndre or adommage[1] you in no manere of wyse, and I, said she, ne shall doo nor thinke to none other thing but in what manere I shall mowe best encresse[2] in worship and honour both you and your lynee.[3] And Raymondin yede[4] & gan sey to her in this manere, Soo shal I do it to the playsire of God."

[1] Hurt.   [2] More best or better increase.   [3] Lineage, or family.   [4] Went.

RAYMONDIN AND MELUSINE AT THE CHAPEL.   [*See p.* 30.

Thus, then, Raymondin and Melusine plighted their troth, and she at once commenced carrying out her portion of the agreement by giving him good advice, as how to act with regard to the death of his uncle. She told him to return to Poitiers, and he was to reply in answer to all questions put to him regarding the Earl his uncle, " Is he not come home again ? " and when they should tell him nay, he was to reply that he never saw him since the chase was at its height, at which time he lost him ; and he must feign to be more surprised at his uncle's absence than any other. She foretold that soon afterwards the hunters of his train, and others of his following, should appear, bringing the corpse, borne upon a litter, and that his wounds should seem to have been made by a boar's teeth, so that all men should say that a wild boar had slain him, and people should reckon it as a great deed to the Earl, for that he had slain so ferocious a beast. He was to go to the funeral, put on mourning as the others did, and wait until it was the time for the barons to do obeisance to their new Earl, Bertrand, when he was to return to the fountain of Soyf, there to find Melusine. But, before his final adieu, she gave him two rings, one of which, as long as he wore it, would keep him harmless from the stroke of any weapon, and the other would give him victory over his enemies.

"Thanne toke Raymondin leve of the lady, and embrased and kyssed her swetly and moche frendly," and went his way, whilst Melusine returned to her sisters. On his arrival at Poitiers everything fell out as predicted, and when, after the funeral, the barons were ordered to come and do obeisance to their new earl, Raymondin dutifully returned to his *fiancée*, but only to find great marvels on his arrival at the trysting-place.

First and foremost, on his coming to the fountain of Soyf, he perceived a chapel which he had never seen before, around which were many knights and ladies, who welcomed him with acclamations, begged him to alight, and to accompany them unto their lady, who was awaiting him in her pavilion. As he went towards it, Melusine came to meet him, and, after some conversation, dinner was announced, and they adjourned to the pavilion for that important meal : and when he asked whence came all this retinue ? was answered that they were all at his command.

She then gave him the following counsel : Premising that the morrow was the day for the barons to do homage to Earl Bertrand, she advised that he, also, should present himself, and that he should ask a boon of the new earl : one not likely to be denied, on account of its apparent modesty. She bade him ask, as a return of services done to his father, neither town, nor castle, nor anything of great value, but only as much land as the hide of a stag would *comprehend.* Of course it is an old story, told of Dido, as of others, but still it is part of the romance, and

RAYMONDIN ASKS A BOON OF THE EARL. [*See p.* 33.

resulted in making our hero, for the first time in his life, a landed proprietor. He was to ask for this land as a free gift, entirely disassociated from rent or homage, and he was also to be careful that this grant should be under the Earl's great seal, and that of his suzerain. She told him, also, that after this interview, the issue of which was undoubted, he should meet a man with a stag's hide in a bag, and this hide he was to buy, without haggling, for whatever price the man chose to ask. He was then to cut it in " the smallest and narowest waye that is possible to be cutte after the maner of a thonge," and then, this purchase being made, and the grant signed, sealed, and delivered, he was to go with proper men to the fountain of Soyf, where he would find the trees cut down, and all ready for him to measure the ground—which, when staked out, if there was any leather over after the circular measurement, he was to take it down the hill. He took an affectionate leave of his lady love, and rode off to Poitiers, where he met with a kindly reception from all.

As an illustration of the manners of the time, I must needs quote a line or two from the MS., showing the intimate connection between the secular and clerical power. "And the next morow they yede[1] all togedre unto Saynt Hylary of Poyters where the devyne servyse was doon right worshypfully. And atte that servyse was

[1] Went.

the yonge Erle revested lyke a Canoyne as theyre prymat or Abbot, and dyde hys devoyre[1] as it apparteyned, and that of custome was for to be doo."

The Barons did their homage, and, when it came to Raymondin's turn, he preferred his request, as he had been instructed, which the Earl gladly granted, and the next day he took his leave, when he met, as Melusine had foretold, a man who asked him, " Sire, wyl ye bye this hertis skynne that I have within my sack for to make good huntyng cordes for yo[r] hunters. By my feyth said Raymondin / ye /[2] yf thou wilt selle it. And at one word what shall I paye for hit. By my feyth, sire, said the man, ye shall paye to me for it ten shelyngs or ellis ye shall not have it. Ffrend sayd thanne Raymondin to the said man, bryng it home with me and I shall pay the there. And he answered with a good wille. Thanne he folowed Raymondin unto his hous and there he delyvered hys hyde, and Raymondin payed hym for it. And anone after, Raymondin sent for a sadelmaker to whom he said, My frend yf it plese you ye muste cutte this hyde in fourme of a thonge in the narowest & smallest wyse that is possible to be doo. The sadler dide cutte it, and after, they leyd it within the sac thus cutte."

On arriving at the Fountain of Soyf he found the trees all levelled—at least, such as were in the way of his

---

[1] Devoir—duty.   [2] Yea, or yes.

RAYMONDIN MEASURES HIS LAND.

measuring ; at which he, naturally, marvelled at first ; but
in this, as in other things, Raymondin seems to have
speedily recognized the guiding hand of a superior genius,
and accepted the situation as he found it. The Romance
omits to state whether there was a commission associated
with Raymondin to execute the Earl's gift, but there evidently was something of the sort, although it is somewhat
indefinitely described as "they." "Whan they that shuld
delyver the gefte¹ saw the hyde cutte so small they were
of it alle abashed, and said to Raymondin that they wyst
not what to doo. And there incontynent came to them
two men clothed with cours cloth, the which said in this
manere. We are come hither for to helpe you. Thanne
they toke out of the sack the hyde, and bare it unto the
bottom of the valley, as nigh the roche² as they coude,
and there they dide sette a stake in the erthe, and to this
stake they fasted the one end of the hyde, and as they
went they set stakes for to hold with the said thonge
rounde aboute the roche, and whan they were come ageyn
to the first stake there was yet a grete remenant of the thong,
and for to sette and fournysshe it, they drew it downward
to the valey, and so far they went with it that they came
to the ende of it. And ye must knowe that after that, it
is said in the countre, and as the very and true history
witnesseth, there sprange at ende of the said thonge, a fayre
fontayn, the which rendred so moche of water, that a ryvere

¹ Gift, or boon.　　　² Rock.

wexed or grew therof. Wherof many a mylle dyde grynde corne, and yet now grynden.[1]   Thanne they that were there sent for to delyvere to Raymondin the place were moche abasshed, as wel of the fontayne that they see spryng sodaynly before them as of the grete compace of the ledder [2] whiche conteyned wel the space of two myll [3] of grounde."

The "they," although they could scarcely understand the matter, faithfully executed their commission, and gave possession to Raymondin of all the land thus acquired, although their astonishment was not decreased by the sudden disappearance of the two men who were so opportunely officious with their help : and, after thanking Earl Bertrand for his kind gift, and acknowledging that it was all done without his knowledge, or interference, he set out to rejoin Melusine. She, having thus provided an estate for her lord, naturally wished to share it with him, and urged their immediate espousal—only—quite properly, and most womanlike—she intended her wedding-day to be *the day* of her life, and that her marriage should be no hole-and-corner proceeding, but done openly and honourably, in the face of day, and with every befitting ceremony. Therefore she enjoined Raymondin to return to the Earl, and invite him, and his mother, to the wedding, and, meantime, she would make all the necessary arrangements for the festival. She was worldly wise enough to instruct

[1] And still do grind.   [2] Leather.   [3] Miles.

MARRIAGE OF RAYMONDIN AND MELUSINE. [See p. 43.

him that he might tell the Earl that he was going to wed
a king's daughter, but more than that he was not to say :
indeed it is difficult to imagine how he could, seeing that
he did not know himself.

The Earl spoke to Raymondin as to the mystery that
shrouded his wife, but the lover was staunch, and per-
tinently replied, " My lord, sith it suffyseth me as thereof
ye oughte wel to be playsed, ffor I take no wyf that shall
brawle or stryve with you, but only with me, and I alone
shall bere eyther joye or sorowe for it." This argument
was unanswerable, and the Earl promised to attend the
marriage ceremony, and bring with him, not only his
mother, but a " foyson " of barons, and, besides his lady,
" many other ladyes and damoyselles."

" On the morowe erly the Erle aroos & herd his masse,
and made the barons to be manded & boden [1] for to goo
with hym to the weddynge of Raymondin, and they cam
incontinent."

When they did arrive they were all amazed at the
magnificence of the preparations, for, on their way, an
old knight and twenty-four horsemen met, and afterwards
escorted them. Then Raymondin and the Earl of Forest
joined the cortége, and they rode merrily to their des-
tination, where " the Erle was lodged within the moost
riche lodgyn that ever he had seen before. After (wards)
evry man was lodged honourably after his estate, &

[1] Warned and bidden.

they said that within theyre owne places at whom [1] they
were not so wel lodged. Theire horses were lodged within
the grett tentes, so at large & at theire ease that no
palfrener [2] was there but that he was full wel playsed.
And alle they marvailled fro whens so moch of good
and such plente of richesses might come there so haboun-
dauntly;" and well they might, for the historian Jean
d'Arras has not spared his imagination.

No touch of mine shall spoil the description of the
wedding. The guests arrived just in time, "and whan
the countesse had rested a lytel while, and that she was
arayed with her ryche rayments, also her doughter
Blanche, Knyghtes & Esquyers, ladyes and damoyselles
of her companye, wente into the chambre of the spouse,
the whiche chambre was fayrer, and passed [3] of ryches
alle the other chambres, but whan they sawe Melusyne
& perceyved her ryche tyres,[4] her riche gowne alle set
w^t precious stones & perlys ; the coler that she had about
her nek, her gerdell, & her other rayments that she had
on her, they alle marvaylled gretly, and specially the
Countesse that sayd consideryng that grete estate,
Never had I wened [5] ne supposed that no queene ne
Emperesse had be in alle the world that might have
founde suche jewellis so riche & so grete in value. . . .
The Erle of Poitiers and one of the moost hygh barons,
that is to wete the Erle of fforest, addressed & ledde the

[1] Home.   [2] Groom.   [3] Surpassed.   [4] Attire, or dress.   [5] Ween, or fancy.

spouse unto the said chapelle of our lady which was so
rychly adorned & arayed so nobly that wonder it was
to see, as of parements,[1] and ornaments of cloth of gold
purfeld [2] & set w[t] perlys and precious stones so wel
wrought, and so connyngly browded [3] that marvaylle it
was to loke on. Fayre ymages straungely kerved,[4] as
of crucifixe & figure of o[r] lady all of pure & fyn gold,
and bokes were there so wel writen, and so riche that
make the world:[5] rycher bokes might not have be.
And there was a bysshop that wedded them & songe
masse before them."

The marriage ceremony over, the bride, bridegroom,
and guests, all adjourned to the pavilions, where a dinner
was served, which, of course, was a marvel of cookery.
All were served on plates of gold, and, as fast as one
course was finished and removed, another was ready to
take its place. The dinner came to an end at last, "the
tables were taken up & graces said, and they were served
with ypocras & spyces," the knights and esquires donned
their armour, and went into the tilting ring, where a
scaffold was erected for Melusine and the ladies. Of
course, in the tourney Raymondin was the victorious
hero, overthrowing all comers; and night brought this
disport to an end.

The close of the evening is such a revelation of 15th

---

[1] Furniture.   [2] Trimmed, or edged.   [3] Embroidered.
[4] Carved.   [5] As rich as could be made in the whole world.

century manners, that it can only be told to the best advantage in the very words of the chroniclers. " And thanne they yede[1] into the grete tente, and after they had washen, they set them at table and wel & richely they were served, and after souper were the tables taken up, and they wesshed theyre hands, & graces were said. This doon the ladyes wente asyde pryvely and toke other gownes on them and cam agayn for to daunse. The feste was fayre, and the worship was there grete, so that the Erle and all they that were come with hym marvaylled gretly of the grette ryches & honour that they sawe there. And whan it was tyme they ledd the spouse to bed most honourably within a wonder (fully) marvayllous & riche pavyllon. And there the Erles of Poitiers & of fforest betoke her unto the ladye's handes. And than the Countess of Poitiers and other grete ladyes had the spouse to bed, and did endoctryne her in suche thynges that she oughte for to doo, howbeit that she was ynough purveyed thereof; but not wythstandyng she thanked them moch humbly therfore. And whan she was abed the ladyes abode thereunto tyme that Raymondin came in."

The gentlemen had not the solace of the smoking-room, but sat chatting over the jousting of the day, until the arrival of a knight with a message from the ladies that it was time for Raymondin to join his bride.

[1] Went.

BLESSING THE NUPTIAL BED.   [See p. 47.

" At this word they went and ledde Raymondin to the pavyllon and soone he was brought to bed. And thanne cam there yᵉ Bysshop that had spoused them and did halowe theyre bed, and, after that, everychon toke his leve, and the courteyns were drawen aboute the bed."

Next morning they all heard mass, " the offertory of whiche was grete and riche," and, after more feasting, the company took their departure, Melusine accompanying the Countess of Poitiers beyond the little town of Columbiers, and, at parting, presenting her with " a fayre & most riche owche ¹ of gold, in value unestimable, and to Blanche her doughter a gerland all set with perlys, with saphirs, rubyes, and with many other precyous stones in grete nombre. And alle they that sawe the said owche and gerland marvaylled gretly of the beaute, goodnes & value of it."

Although the most noble of the guests had departed, still plenty more took their places, and the feasting went on right merrily. At length the festivity came to an end, and the young married couple were left to themselves. Melusine, who took upon herself the ordering of everything, and, from a business point of view, seems to have regarded Raymondin as simply a sleeping partner, immediately set to work to build a castle on their small estate, and, under her potent influence, it rose in a marvellously short space of time. "And every Saturday

¹ Brooch.

Melusyne payed truly her werkmen, and mete and drynke they hadde in haboundance ; but trouth it is, that no body knew from whens these werkmen were."

The castle being built, of course there was a house-warming—needless to say, in Melusine's large-hearted and open-handed manner, a somewhat extravagant festival. The Earls of Poitiers and Forest were, of course, present, and jousting and feasting fully occupied the time and attention of all. Melusine asked them kindly to name her castle, but good manners forbade it, and the Earl of Poitiers politely pointed out that none was so worthy to christen the château as the fair châtelaine and founder. " Ha, ha, my lord, said Melusyne, sith it ne may none otherwise be, and that I see your playsire is that I gyve name to it, hit shal be called after myn owne name Lusignen. By my feyth sayd the Erle the name fetteth full wel to it for two causes, ffirst bycause ye are called Melusyne of Albanye, whyche name in grek langage is as moche for to say, a thyng marvayllous or comyng from grete marveylle—and also this place is bylded and made marvayllously, ffor I beleve not otherwyse, but that as longe as the world shal laste shall there be founde som wonder & marvayllous thinge. Thanne they alle ansuered in this maner. My lord, no man in the world might gyve betre name that bettre shuld fette to it than she hath, as after manere of the place, also the interpretyng made by you of her owne name, and on this oppynyon & worde were alle of one acorde. Whiche name within few days was so publyed that it was knowen through alle the land, and yet at this day it is called soo." The feast came to an end, and the guests departed.

The next important event in the life of Raymondin and Melusine was the birth of their first-born son, Uryan, or Urien. She was unfortunate in her progeny; they were all, in some way or other, malformed. Urien was " moche fayre and wel proporcyoned or shapen in all hys membres, except hys vysage that was short and large, one ey he had rede and the other blew. He was baptysed & named Uryan, and wete [1] it that he had the gretest eerys [2] that ever were seen on eny child of his age, and when they were outdrawen they were as grete as the handling of a fan."

Melusine found her husband some employment in visiting his relations at Brut, Brittany, and, while he was away, she built a city as a surprise for him on his return. She then gave birth to a son, who was christened Edon, and his face was red. She then built the towns and castles of Melle, Donant, and Mernant, and afterwards the city and tower of St. Maxence, besides commencing the abbey there.

She then bore a third son, named Guyon, or Guy, but he had one eye higher than the other; after which she amused herself with building the town and castle of Parthenay, and also founded the port and city of Rochelle,

[1] Know.　　　　[2] Ears.

as well as many other towns.   Her fourth child was
named Anthony, " but in his birth he brought a token
along hys chyk ¹ that was the foot of a lyon, whereof
they that sawe hym wondred, & moche were abasshed."

In the seventh year of her married life she bore her
fifth boy, who was named Raynold; but his defect was
that he only had one eye, but that must have been of
telescopic power, for he could see ships as far out at sea
as one-and-twenty leagues.   The year after she was
brought to bed of a son who, afterwards, was famous in
chronicle.   He " had to name Geffray, whiche at hys
birth brought in hys mouthe a grete & long toth ² that
apyered ³ without an ench long & more, & therfore
men added to his propre name Geffray with the grete
toth ; and he was moch grete & hye & wel formed &
strong marveyllously hardy & cruel, in so moche that
every man fered & dradde hym whan he was in (of) age."

The year following, her son Fromond was born, whose
deformity was the having a bunch of hair on his nose.   He
was very devout and turned monk, and was burnt, with all
the other monks, by his brother Geoffrey with the great
tooth, when he sacked and burnt the abbey of Maillières.
Her next maternal effort was a rank failure, for this son
" brought at hys birth thre eyen,⁴ one of the which was
in the mydel of his forhed.   He was so evyl & so cruel
that at the foureth yere of hys age he slew two of hys

---

¹ Cheek.   ² Tooth.   ³ Stuck out.   ⁴ Eyes.

nourryces." His name was very properly " Horrible."
She also had two younger children, Raymond and
Theodorik, but there seems to have been very little the
matter with their personal appearance.

With the fortunes of these children we have nothing
to do, except inasmuch as they come in contact with
the story of their father and mother ; who seem to have
lived thoroughly happy and prosperous lives until such
time as Raymondin's brother, the Earl of Forest, came
one day to pay them a visit, and was received with all
the courtesy that the pair could show him. His re-
quital of this kindness was the wrecking of their love—and
domestic happiness. He arrived on a Saturday, the day
when Melusine was "not at home," and when he and
Raymondin were going to dinner he asked after his
sister-in-law, marvelling at her absence. Raymondin,
who took his wife's weekly absence as a matter of course,
calmly replied that she was not then visible, but next
day she would be there to welcome his brother. " But
for that ansuere the Erle of Fforest held not hys peas,
but thus said agen to hys brother. Ye are my brother,
I owe[1] not to hyde to you your dyshono^r. Now fayre
brother wete[2] it that the comyn[3] talking of the peple is
that Melusyne yor wyf evry saturday in the yere is with
another man in avoultyre, & so blynd ye are by her
sayeng, that ye dare not enquere, nor knoweth wher she

[1] Ought.   [2] Know.   [3] Common.

be cometh or goeth ; and also, others sayen & make them strong that she is a spryghte of the fayry that on evry Saturday maketh her penaunce. I wot not to whiche of bothe I shal byleve, and for none other cause I am com hither but to advertyse [1] you therof."

This information, given, possibly, with every good intention, naturally disturbed Raymondin, who had hitherto taken his wife's hebdomadal absences with perfect calmness, and as strictly in the proper nature of things. But at this revelation, that his wife's conduct was common talk, he abruptly rose from table and retired to his chamber, where he became the prey of terrible jealousy. After some self-communion, like a man he determined to know the worst ; he "toke his swerd & girded it about hym, and went toward the place where as Melusyne went evry Saturday in the yer ; and when he cam there he fond a doore of yron thikk & strong, and wete it wel, he had never betofore that tyme so ferre thitherward ; and whan he perceyved the doore of yron, he toke hys swerd that was hard & tempered w^t fyn stele, and w^t the poynte of it dyde so moche that he perced the doore and made a holl in it, and loked in at that holl, and sawe there Melusyne that was within a grete bathe of marbel stone,[2] where were steppis to mounte in it, and was wel XV foot of length, and therein she bathed herself makyng there her penytence."

[1] Let you know.   [2] See Frontispiece.

It was then he made the discovery of the awful effects of his wife's fairy origin, and of the expiation she was doomed to undergo. Doubtless he regretted his indiscreet curiosity, especially when " he sawe Melusyne within the bathe unto her navell in forme of a woman kymbyng her heere, and from the navel downward in lyknes of a grete serpent, the tayll as grete & thykk as a barell and so long it was that she made it to touche oftymes, while that Raymondin beheld her the rouf of the chambre that was ryght hye."

The manuscript gives some long and very doleful soliloquies of Raymondin, who went home, and to bed, in a state of mind easier to be imagined than described. With the first flush of dawn Melusine returned, as was her wont, to her home, and the description of the meeting between husband and wife in the MS. is so quaint that the story would suffer much were it not told in its very words. " Ere sayth thistorye that in such dole[r] & bewaylynge abode Raymondin al that nyght tyl it was day lyght. And as soone as aurora might be perceyved, Melusyne came & entred in to the chambre, and whan Raymondin herd her com, he made semblant[1] of slepe. She toke of her clothes and than al naked layed herself by hym. And thenne bygan Raymondin to syghe, as that he felt grete doleur[2] at herte, and Melusyne embraced hym & asked what hym eyled,[3] sayeng in this wyse.

[1] Feigned.   [2] Grief.   [3] Ailed—was the matter with him.

My lord what eyleth you, be ye syke. And whan Raymondin sawe that she of none other thing spake, he supposed that she nothyng had knowen of this faytte,[1] but for nought he byleved so,[2] ffor she wyst wel that he had not shewn the matere to no man, wherfor she suffred at that tyme, & made no semblant therof, wherfore he was right joyous and ansuered to her. Madame I have be (en) somwhat evyl at ease & have had an ager.[3] My lord sayd Melusyne abasshe you not, ffor yf it plese God ye shal soone be hole. And thenne he that was right joyous said to her. By my feyth, swete love, I fele me wel at ease for your comyng; and she said, I am therof glad, and whan tyme requyred they roos, and went to here masse, and soone after was the dyner redy."

Thus, for the moment, no harm came of Raymondin's discovery, and the pair lived in loving amity until an unusual escapade on the part of their son Geoffrey with the great tooth led to most disastrous effects. It arose in this wise: His brother Fromond had a liking to lead a clean and godly life, and, after some opposition on his father's part, he entered into religious life as a monk at the abbey of Maillières. This, the warrior Geoffrey looked upon as a degradation to his family and lineage; none of them ever had been shavelings, none of them ever should be, or he would know the reason why; so he at once started off "with grete yre agenste the Abbot

---

[1] Fact.　　[2] He knew not the facts of the case.　　[3] Ague.

GEOFFREY WITH THE GREAT TOOTH BURNING THE ABBEY OF MAILLIÈRES.
[See p. 58.

& convent of Maylesses ; and at that tyme the said abbot
& his monkes were in chapitre, and Geffray then coming
to the place, entred with swerd gird about hym in to
the chapitre. And whan he perceyved the abbot & hys
monkes he said al on hye [1] to them. Ye false monkes,
how have ye had the hardynes to have enchanted my
· brother in so moche that thrughe your false & subtyl
langage have shorne hym monke ; by the teeth of God
yl ye thought it, ffor ye shal drynk therfore of an evyl
drynk."

"Helas my lord, said th'abbot, for the love of God
have mercy on us and suffre you to be enfourmed of the
trouth & rayson, for on my Creator, I nor none of us all
counseylled hym never thereto. Thenne cam Froymont
foorth, that trowed wel to have peased the yre [2] of
Geffray hys brother, and thus said. My dere brother,
by the body & sowle which I have gyven to god, here
is no personne, nor within this place that ever spake
any word to me touching my profession, ffor I have it
doon of myn owne free wylle & thrugh devocion. By
my sowle, said Geffray, so shalt thou be therfore payed
with the others, for it shal not be wytted [3] me to have
a brother of myn a monke, and with these words he
went out of the Chapter and shetted the doores fast
after hym & closed the Abbot & the monkes therynne,

---

[1] In a loud tone of voice.   [2] Believed he could appease the wrath.
[3] I will not be twitted.

and incontinent he made al the meyne [1] of the place
to bryng there wode & strawe ynough al about the
Chapter, and fyred it, & sware he shuld brene them all
therynne, & that none shuld escape. Thenne came the
ten knyghtes foorth tofore [2] Geffray, whiche blamed hym
of that horryble faytte, sayeng that Froymond his brother
was in good purpos, & that happly throughe hys prayers
& good dedes the sowles of hys frendes & others myght
be asswaged & holpen. By the teeth of God, sayd
thenne Geffray, nother he nor none monke in this place
shal never syng masse nor say prayers but they shal
all be bruled [3] & brent."

His ten knights left him, for they would not have aught
to do with such a diabolical scheme; but their defection
in no way hindered Geoffrey from his design, and with
his own hand he fired the abbey. The chronicler says:
" It was a pyteous syght, ffor as soone as the monkes
sawe the fyre they bygan to crye piteously & to make
bytter & doulourous bewaylyngs, but al that prevaylled
them nought." In fine, Fromond and all the monks were
burnt, and then the fiend in human shape, Geoffrey with
the great tooth, began to feel compunction, and to repent him as far as his evil disposition would allow; but
the mischief was done, and the poor monks could never
be restored to life.

Ill news flies apace; and it was not long before a

[1] Servants.   [2] Towards.   [3] Burnt, from the French *brûler*, to burn.

messenger came to Raymondin with the tidings of his
son's murder of his inoffensive brother. He refused to
believe the news, but on the messenger offering to be
put in prison and hanged, if it were not true, he mounted
his horse and set off at full speed for Maillières; nor did
he draw rein until he came there, where he found even
as the messenger had said. Turning the matter over in
his mind, he could come but to one conclusion, after his
discovery of his wife's peculiarity, and at once laid the
blame on her shoulders. " I byleve it is but fantosme or
spryght-werke of this woman, and as I trowe, she never
bare no child that shal at the ende have perfection, ffor
yet hath she brought none but that it hath som strange
token. See I not the horrybyllnes of her son called
horryble that passed not vij yere of age whan he slew
two squyers of myn, and, or ever he was thre yere old, he
made dye two gentyl women his nourryces through hys
bytting of theyre pappes. Sawe I not also theyre moder
on that Saturday whan my brother of Fforest to me
brought evyl tydyngs of her, in fourme of a serpent from
the navel downward ; by god, yea, and wel I wote certayn
that it is som spryght, some fantosme or Illusyon that thus
hath abused me, ffor the first tyme that I sawe her, she
knew & coude reherce all my fortune & aventure."

Pondering in this wise, "pensefull & wroth," he rode
homewards, and it may be easily imagined that his
meeting with Melusine was not of a loving character.

She was not unprepared for it, for the barons had sent
a messenger to her, telling her of all that had passed,
and she at once left, with all her retinue, for Lusignan,
"and there she sojourned by the space of thre dayes, &
ever she was of symple & hevy contenaunce, and went al
about in the place up & doun, here & there, gyvyng
ofte syghes so grete that it was mervaylle & pyteous to
here." And this grief, the chronicler thinks, was not only
due to the death of one son, and the outrageous conduct
of the other, but to the knowledge ("whiche I byleve be
trew") of her own impending calamity.

Their meeting was painful in the extreme. On her
part nothing was omitted to welcome her lord. The
room chosen was the fairest in the house, looking over
the pleasure gardens and the beautiful prospect which
stretched for miles round; and she herself made her
appearance, "accompanyed of many ladyes & noble
damoyselles, & of the barons of the land. . . . Thenne
whan she sawe Raymondin, humbly & ryght honourably
salued[1] hym, but thenne he was so dolaunt[2] & replenysshed with yre that he to her ansuered never a
word." But she, caring little for his black looks, spoke
to him very sensibly on the subject; blaming Geoffrey's
diabolical behaviour, but reminding her husband that the
past could not be undone, and the best thing was to make
reparation for the sin and outrage committed, and hope

[1] Saluted.   [2] Doleful.

THE FAINTING OF MELUSINE.

[See p. 63.

that Geoffrey might so amend his life as to be a shining example of all the virtues in the future.

Raymondin, although in his heart he could not but confess the justice of her reasoning, was so "replenysshed and perced with yre, that al rayson natural was fled & goon from hym," and he at once began a violent abuse of his devoted wife, commencing with "Go thou hens, fals serpente," and saying that she and all her children, save Fromond, were of the devil. Either the violence of this public attack, or the fact of her secret being thus divulged, had such an effect upon Melusine, that she fell to the ground in a swoon, so deathly, that for half an hour she did not breathe, and was pulseless. Cold water vigorously applied, and other remedies, at length brought her round, and restored her to her senses, when she gently upbraided her husband with the revelation of her dual existence, which had so abruptly put an end to the fond dream of her life, that she might have lived the allotted time of mortal existence, and then have been buried in the Church of Our Lady of Lusignan, whereas now she would have to resume her fairy shape of half serpent, half woman, and linger about in that guise until the day of judgment. The thoughts of this dreadful fate had such an effect upon the pair that they both fainted, and then wept and bewailed both barons and damoiselles, " and they al lamented and bewaylled so pyteously & rendered teerys in habundance, in so moche that it was a pyteous syght."

When they came to life again, Melusine spoke as to her testamentary wishes in a somewhat prophetic strain. She told Raymondin that during his lifetime he should hold all his possessions in peace, because she would watch over him, but that his heirs would have trouble to maintain them in the time to come. That he must not banish Geoffrey, for that he would become a good and useful member of society. She desired that of her two youngest children, Raymond and Theodorik, the former should be Earl of Forest, and the younger Lord of Parthenay, Vernon, and Rochelle, with the port there. All the others were quite able to take care of themselves, except the awful child " Horrible," who, she said, would, if allowed to live, commit more wickedness than any other man ; therefore she desired, after she was gone, that he should be put to death—a suggestion that was duly attended to, and he was comfortably stifled with smoke from wet hay, and then honourably buried. She regretted having to quit her human form, and all that made life dear to her, but was somewhat comforted by the fact that she should still be able to see her husband, although he might not be able to behold her. She gave her husband two rings, which seem to have been identical with those she bestowed on him in the time of their courtship ; told him that she was the daughter of King Elynas of Albany and of his queen Pressyne, recapitulated her testamentary wishes, and, having heaved " a sore syghe," she flew out of the window into the air, " transfigured lyke a serpent grete & long in XV foote of lengthe.

THE FLIGHT OF MELUSINE.

"And wete it wel that on the basse[1] stone of the wyndowe apereth at this day th' emprynte of her foot serpentous.[2] Then encreased the lamentable sorowes of Raymondin, and of the barons, ladyes, and damoyselles, and moost in especial Raymondin's hevynes above al other. And forthwith they loked out of the wyndowe to beholde what way she toke. And ye noble Melusyne so transfygured as it is aforsaid flyeing thre tymes about the place passed foreby the wyndowe gyvyng at everyche tyme an horryble cry & pyteous that caused them that beheld her to wepe for pyte, ffor they perceyved wel that loth she was to departe fro the place, and that it was by constraynte. And thenne she toke her way toward Lusynen, makyng in th'ayre by her furyousnes suche horryble crye & noyse that it semed al th'ayer to be replete with thundre & tempeste.

" Thus as I have shewed went Melusyne lyke a serpent flyeing in th'ayer toward Lusynen, and not so hygh but that the men of the Counte[3] might see her, and she was herd a myle in th'ayer, ffor she made suche noyse that al the peple was abasshed. And so she flawgh[4] to Lusynen thre tymes about the ffortres cryeng so pyteously & lamentably lyke the voyce of a mermayde. Wherof they of the ffortresse & of the toun were gretly abasshed, and wyst not what they shuld thinke, ffor they sawe the figure of a serpent

[1] Window-sill.
[2] A serpent's foot must have been remarkable—reminding one of the old carol wherein Joseph was invited to "sit upon a serpent's knee."
[3] County, or district.   [4] Flew.

and the voyce of a woman that cam from the serpent. And
whan she had floughe about the ffortresse thre tymes she
lyghted so sodaynly & horribly upon the toure called
posterne, bryngyng with her suche thundre & tempeste
that it semed that bothe the fortres & the tour shuld have
sonk & fallen, & therwith they lost the syght of her and
wyst not where she was be come. . . . And (when) the
tydyngs were knowen in the Countre the poure peuple
made grete lamentacion & sorowe, and wysshed her agen
with pyteous syghes, ffor she had doo[1] them grete good.
And then bygan the obsequyes of her to be observyd in al
abbeyes & churches that she had founded, and Raymondin
her lord dede to be doon[2] for her almesses[3] & prayers
thrugh al his land."

This was a fitting tribute to her worth and goodness, and
her memory, or rather the tradition, of her existence still
remains in the neighbourhood of Poitiers, where to this
day a sharp and sudden cry is called a " cri de Melusine,"
and, at fair times, Melusine cakes are sold—half woman
half serpent. The legend goes on to say that she used to
come at night to visit her two little ones, " and held them
tofore the fyre and eased them as she coude ;[4] and wel
sawe the nourryces that, who durst no word speke. And
more encreced the two children in nature in a weke than
dide other children in a moneth, wherof the peuple had
grete marvayll, but when Raymondin knew it by the

[1] Done.　[2] Caused to be done.　[3] Alms, or charities.　[4] Well as she was able.

nourryces that Melusyne cam there evry nyght to vysyte her children, relessed [1] his sorowe, trustyng to have her agen, but that thoughte was for nought ; ffor never after sawe her in forme of a woman, howbeit divers have sith [2] sen her in femenyn figure. And wete it that how (ever) wel Raymondin hoped to have her ageyn, nevertheles he had alway suche herty sorowe that there is none that can tell it. And there was never man sith that sawe hym laugh nor make Joye."

He had, however, a profound hatred of his son Geoffrey, and the latter went away, doing useful work. He killed a giant, and released his prisoners, found the tomb of his grandfather and grandmother, after which he devoted his energies to the slaughter of his uncle, the Earl of Forest, whom he rightly deemed the *fons et origo* of all the misfortunes that happened to his mother. Having chased the unfortunate Earl, sword in hand, all through the castle, on to its roof, the unhappy nobleman, in an endeavour to escape, missed his footing, fell, and was killed. Raymondin thought this was carrying filial duty quite far enough, and said, " I must (ap)pease Geffray or he do any more dommage." So he sent the young Theodorik to bid him come and see him. He did so, and begged his father's forgiveness. Nay, more, he promised to rebuild the abbey of Maillières, far more magnificently than it had previously been, and to provide for ten monks in excess of the original

[1] Relieved. [2] Since.

number. After rebuking his too zealous son, Raymondin told him he was going on a journey, and would therefore leave him in sole charge of his possessions, with the exception of the arrangement entered into in accordance with Melusine's wishes.

This settled, he set out for Rome, where he interviewed the Pope, named Benedictus, who received him kindly— heard his confession, gave him penance, and had him afterwards to dinner. Raymondin informed his Holiness of his intention to retire to a hermitage at Montserrat, in Aragon, and obtained the papal license so to do. Meanwhile Geoffrey's conscience smote him sorely; and, troubled by the recollection of his misdeeds, he also determined to go to Rome, see the Pope, confess his sins, and suffer his punishment. This he did, and the Holy Father, among many other penances, ordered him to rebuild the abbey of Maillières and provide for a hundred and twenty monks. Matters thus being accommodated, he expressed his intention of finding his father, and the Pope directed him where to go.

He duly found Raymondin, who, when he knew that Geoffrey's repentance was sincere, took him in his arms and kissed him, at the same time declaring his unalterable intention to die a hermit, and insisting on his son's return to Lusignan. On his arrival there, the barons did him homage as their new Earl, and he then rebuilt the abbey of Maillières.

We hear of Melusine yet again, for the chronicler tells us " that as long as Raymondin lyved Geffray & Theodoryk came there every yere ones to see hym, but it befell on a day that they were both at Lusynen redy for to go to Mountserrat, a marvayllous aventure ; ffor there was seen upon the batelments of the Castel, a grete & horryble serpent, the which cryed with a femenyn voys, whereof all the people was abasshed, but wel they wyst that it was Melusine. Whan the bretheren beheld it, teerys in habundance bygan to fall from their eyen, ffor they knew wel that it was their moder. And whan the serpent sawe them wepe, she enclyned the heed toward them, casting such an horryble cry & so dolorous that it semed (to) them that herd it that the ffortres shuld have fall(en)."

Alarmed at this portent, the two sons set out on their journey, only to find their father dead. They did all that was possible under the circumstances, went into mourning, with all their retinue, and gave him a magnificent funeral, at which were present the King and Queen of Aragon, and all the nobility of the land.

Here, virtually, the story of Melusine ends, but there are legends arising out of it, besides the deeds of prowess done by her sons—such as her birth, and the fate of herself and sisters. They were the daughters of King Helmas or Helymas of Albania, and his wife Pressyne, who was a fairy. A difficulty seems always to attend the union of a mortal and a supernatural being, and this case was no

exception. Fairies must evidently have their moments of
retreat, far away from spying eyes, and Queen Pressyne
bargained, before marriage, that, whilst she lay in childbed,
her husband should never see her, nor inquire after her.
The promise was given, and of course broken, the penalty
being the vanishing of the fairy wife with her three
daughters, Melusine, Melior, and Palestine. They were
brought up at Avalon in fairy-land, and when they had
arrived at years of discretion, *i.e.*, were fifteen years old,
their mother confided to them the secret of their birth.
The three girls were highly indignant with their father for
his treatment of their mother, and, with the unreasoning
impetuosity of youth, they took summary means to punish
him by enclosing him in a mountain. At his death his
wife buried him sumptuously, but his tomb was hidden
from all men, until discovered, as already told, by his
grandson Geoffrey. But she punished her daughters for
their conduct. We all know Melusine's sad fate; let us
trace that of Melior.

Now it came to pass, after the death of Raymondin's son,
Guyon, who was King of Armenia, there was one of his
descendants who filled his throne, fair to look upon, hardy,
and chivalrous, and it was reported to him that in Great
Armenia was "a Castel whereat was the most fayre lady that
men wyst at that tyme, in al the world. The whiche lady
had a sperhauk,[1] and to al knyghts of noble extraction that

        [1] Sparrowhawk.

thither went, & coude watche the said sperhauk duryng the space of thre dayes and thre nyghts without slepe, the lady should appere tofore them, and gyve them suche worldly gefte as they wold wysshe, and were desyryng to have, except only herself."

These were the terms, simple enough, as it would seem, but very hard to attain (but three only having gained their wishes), for even knights of noble extraction were only made of flesh and blood, and Melior's beauty so vanquished them, that almost invariably they succumbed, and asked her love ; whereon a sad fate overtook them, and she meted out unsparing punishment ; generally, that they should remain her prisoners until the day of judgment. Another condition was attached, that this castle was only to be visited once a year, and that was the day before the vigil of Saint John, and on the morrow of Saint John's Day every man must depart thence.

The king accepted the adventure, and, in due time, came to the castle, where he was met by an old man clothed in white, who, after interrogating the king on his errand, showed him into the castle, which excited his admiration by the splendour of its fittings—which may be imagined from the following description of the sparrowhawk's perch. "And after hym entred the kyng that perceyved in the myddst of the hall a long horne of a unicorn [1] that was fayre

[1] A royal gift from one potentate to another, having no money value, but inestimable as medicine, or as an amulet by means of which poison might be discovered.

& whyte, and therupon was spred a grete cloth of gold, wheron stod the sperhauk, and a glove of whyte sylk under his feet."

The old man clearly explained the conditions, and left his Majesty, who, finding, amongst other things, that a splendid repast was awaiting him, ate thereof, but cautiously and sparingly, as the chronicle sets forth. " Kept good dyete, and made none exces, ffor wel he knew that to moch meet and drynk causeth the body to be pesaunt [1] and slepy." His moderation stood him in good stead, for he achieved his task of watching the bird, without sleeping, for three days and nights ; and his reward came, when, on the fourth day, Melior presented herself. Of course her dazzling beauty, and the lavish wealth everywhere displayed, "gretely abasshed " the king, but she soon set him at his ease. Foolishly, very foolishly, he asked the hand of the lady, but she, probably because she was of kin to him, although rebuking him angrily, yet gave him another chance to retrieve his error.

Still, however, bewitched by her beauty, he asked for herself only, and yet once more she gave him a chance to recant his choice, telling him her history ; that she was of kin to him, and that Holy Church would not suffer their union, and, as a punishment, she prophesied evil to himself and his heirs, and that their estate should fall into decay. Blinded by his infatuation, "he wold have taken the lady

[1] Heavy.

THE KING'S PUNISHMENT.

[*See p.* 77.

by maner of vyolens & by force ; but soon Melyor vanysshed,
that he wyst never where she was become," thus proving
that fairies are fully able to hold their own against vile
man.

The king's punishment swiftly followed his fault. Im-
mediatly after the departyng of Melyor, there fell upon
the Kyng gret & pesaunt strokes as thykk as rayn falleth
from the skye, wherof he was al so brused in every part of
his body, and was drawn by the feet from the halle unto
the barrers [1] without the Castel." He never saw his enemies,
but when he came to shake himself together, and look at
his rueful case, his armour all dinted and broken, and
himself a mass of bruises, he cursed a thousand times the
man whoever brought him the first tidings of this adventure,
and sailed, a sadder and a sorer man, to his own dominions,
and afterwards all fell out as Melior had predicted. This
seems to have been the last ever heard of her.

Her sister Palestine's fate was to be shut up in a
place in Aragon, where she sat for ever guarding her
father's treasures, which could only be attained by one of
his lineage. Many noble knights essayed the task of
rescuing the fabulous riches which were under her guardian-
ship, but none ever returned, being killed by the serpents,
dragons, and other fearsome beasts which guarded it. But
Geoffrey, in his old age, hearing of the disappearance of an
English knight who was of Tristram's line, who foolishly

[1] Barriers.

engaged in this quest, determined to attempt it himself, but his time for such adventures was past, and he died before he could accomplish it.

But Melusine was not easily disposed of, for Jean d'Arras relates several of her recent appearances, authenticating them as well as any modern ghost story could possibly be. One is of a knight named Gersnell, who was keeping the castle of Lusignan, as lieutenant for the King of England, at the time when John, Duc of Berry and Auvergne, besieged it, who "sayd to hym after the reduccyon of the ffortres, that thre days tofore that he gaf it up, he lyeng in hys bed with a woman, hys concubine, named Alexaundryne, perceyved a grete & horryble serpent in the myddle of the chambre, wherof he was gretly abasshed & sore agast, and wold have taken the swerd to have descharged it upon the serpent, but Alexaundrine said thenne to hym in this manyere. Ha valyaunt Gersnell, how ofte have I sene your mortal enemyes tofore your presence, that never ye were aferd, and now for a serpent of femenyn nature ye shake for fere. Wete it for trouth that this serpent is the lady of this place & she that edyfyed it, she shal by no manere wise hurt nor dommage you, but so ferre I understand by her apparysshing that needs ye shal hastly delyvere & gyve up this ffortres to the Duc of Berry. And moreover, said the said Gersnell to my said lord, that hys concubyne fered nothyng the serpent, but that he was never in his dayes so aferd. And that he sawe thenne the said serpent tourned into a forme of a woman clothed in a gowne of cours cloth, & gyrded with a grete corde undernethe the pappes of her, and soone after tourned herselfe in the figure of a serpent and so vanysshed away."

Also, as if this were not sufficient, a man named Godart, who lived within the fortress, swore on the Gospels that he had many times seen the said serpent upon the walls, and she never meddled with him. And to make the case stronger, one Guyon of Wales deposed that on the night the apparition appeared to Gersnell, he also saw it upon the battlements of the dongeon keep.

Can any one doubt the truth of the story after this? Reader, do you?

❡ Here begynneth the history of the va=
lyent knyght, Syr Isenbras.

7

Sir Isumbras

IS peculiarly an English Romance—at least we know of
no version in a foreign tongue, and, indeed, those in
English are very scarce. Three MSS. are known
to exist, all of the 15th century, one at Lincoln, in the
Thornton Collection ; another in the library of Caius
College, Cambridge ; and a third is in the British Museum
(Cotton, Caligula, A. ii.). These have been published—the
first *in extenso*—but the language is very archaic, so that
I have preferred taking the first printed copy I could find,
and that is one printed by William Copland. Black letter,
no date, but in the British Museum Catalogue it is approximately given as 1550. This edition fulfilled most of the
conditions I required. Any one with a very slight knowledge of Old English could read it easily, and, although
it varies in its language from the MSS., it is in complete
accord with them as to the story.

The frontispiece is evidently much older than the
printing, as the wood-block of the knight is both worm-

eaten and broken. It served its purpose, however, as it had already done duty as frontispiece for Sy^r Bevys of Hampton, published by the same printer.

Of all the nobles of his time, Sir Isumbras seems to have been the most favoured. Of specially comely person, great strength, and prowess in arms, wealthy, and yet liberal of his wealth, with a beautiful wife and three lovely children—a happier existence could hardly be imagined ; and so the old chronicler seems to have thought when he wrote.

> Ye shall well heare of a knight
> That was in warre full wyght,[1]
> And doughtye[2] of his dede.
> Hys name was syr Isenbras,
> Man nobler than he was,
> Lyved none with breade.
> He was lyvely, large and longe,
> With shoulders broade, and armes stronge
> That myghtie was to se.
> He was a hardy man and hye,
> All men hym loved that hym se,
> For a gentyll knight was he.
> Harpers loved him in hall,
> With other minstrels all,
> For he gave them golde and fee.
> He was as curtoise as men might thinke,
> Lyberall of meate and drynke
> In the worlde was none so fre.
> He hade a ladye full of beautye
> And also full of charitie ·
> As any lady might be.

[1] Active.   [2] Brave.

Betwene them thay had chyldren thre,
Fayrer forms myght no man se
Under the cope of heaven.

This reads somewhat like the perfection of human
bliss, and so it might have been, had not Sir Isumbræs
lacked some spiritual essentials, which, in all probability,
was owing to his worldly prosperity and happiness. He
was puffed up with pride, and never thought of the Giver
of all things, who had so bounteously bestowed His
favours upon him ; and God thought it necessary, for the
knight's soul's sake, and for the salutary lesson to be
learned from the example he intended to make of him,
to chasten him for his pride and bring him low.

So, after, it befell on a daye
That this knyght went him to playe
Hys forest for to se.
As he loked up on hye
He sawe an aungell in the skye
Which toward hym dyd flye.
Isenbras, he sayde there,
Thou hast forgotten what thou were
For pryde, and golde, and fee.
Wherfore our lord sayth to thee so
All thy good[s] thou must forego
As thou shalt hereafter se.
The worldes welth shall fro the[1] fall,
Thou shalt lose thy children all,
And all thy landes free.
Thy lady goodlyest of all,
For feare of fyre shall flye thy hall
This daye or thou her se.

[1] From thee.

The knyghte fell doune upon his kne
Underneth an Olyve tre
And helde up both his handes.
And then agayne thus sayde he
Lorde God in trinitie
Welcome be thy soundes.
While I am yonge, I maye well go,
When I am olde, I may not so,
Though that I fayne woulde.
Therfore Jesu I pray thee
In youth send me adversitie,
And not when I am olde.
The aungel toke from thence his flight,
And left alone that carefull knyght ;
From hym he wente his waye.

Swift was the divine punishment ; for no sooner was
the angel gone, than his strong steed dropped down dead
from under him, and his hawks and hounds suddenly
expired, and in this plight nought was left for him but
to take his sad way homeward on foot, whilst the tears
streamed down his cheeks. On his way he was met by
some of his household, who had but sad news to give him :
how that all his cattle had been destroyed by adders,
that worms had killed his capons, and that he had no
beast left for the plough, they having died from the effects
of thunder. He took their news with becoming resignation and bade them pass on. Sad-hearted, he still bent his
steps homeward, when he was met by "a lytle lad" who
told him the grievous news that all his castle, &c., was
burned to the ground, and that many of his people had
been killed. In fact the only lives saved were those of

his wife and children who had fled for fear of the fire. When he reached the scene of the catastrophe he found it even as it had been reported unto him.

> A dolefull sight than gan he se,
> Hys wyfe and his chyldren thre
> Out of the fyre were fled.
> There they sate under a thorne
> Bare and naked as they wer borne,
> Brought out of theyr bed.

He took off his "surcoat of pallade"[1] and put it on his wife, cut his scarlet mantle into three pieces in which to wrap his children, and, being fully imbued with the awful punishments with which God had thought good to afflict him, he suggested to his wife that they should at once set out on a pilgrimage to the Holy Land, and visit Calvary. This resolution they carried into effect at once, but in a very meek and lowly fashion.

> The lorde and the ladye bende[2]
> Toke theyr way for to wende
> Upon the same daye.
> Whan that they departe shoulde
> For them wept both yonge and olde,
> Both wyfe, wydow, man and maye.[3]
> They bare with them no maner of thynge
> That was worth a farthynge,
> Cattell, golde ne fe.[4]
> But mekely they asked theyr meate
> Where that they myght it gette
> For saynct charytie.

[1] A rich kind of cloth. [2] Bowed to circumstances. [3] Maid. [4] Nor property.

In this humble manner they passed through " seven
lands " safely, sometimes subsisting on the alms of the
charitable ; at others, only on berries, and the tender
shoots of the thorn.   At length they came to a river,
through which Sir Isumbras waded, with his eldest child
in his arms, and, having placed him under a bush of broom,
he re-crossed the river to fetch his second born; but, whilst
he was in mid stream, a lion bore away his eldest boy,
and a leopard took his next child, who was with his
mother.

After the first burst of grief they piously bowed to the
will of the Creator, and pursued their journey through a
forest, until they came to the sea shore, where they saw a
fleet of " thre hundred shyppes and mo," belonging to the
Soudan of the Saracens, who was there in person.   As
they had tasted neither meat nor drink for seven days,
they not unnaturally agreed to pay the Soudan a visit,
and ask for some provisions.   But the Soudan thought
they were spies, and ordered them to be beaten and sent
away.   Their pitiful case, however, was apparent to the
bystanders, and caused much commiseration among them.

> A knyght kneled before the kynge
> And sayd it is a pytifull thynge
> That poore penaunce to se.
> He semeth a man so gentyll and fre,
> Though he be in necessitie,
> It is ruth[1] and pytie.

[1] Compassion should be shown him.

> His eyen are gray as any glasse ;
> Were he as well fedde as ever he was
> Like a knight shoulde he be.
> Hys wyfe as wyte as whalesbone,
> Though she with weping be overgone,
> She is as white as blosome on tre.

This intercession had weight with the Soudan, and he ordered the wayfarers to be brought before him, which was done, after they had been fed and clothed. He was struck with Sir Isumbras's personal appearance, and offered to dub him a knight if he would go and fight for him, first of all renouncing Christianity and embracing the faith of Mahound. But this was too much for Sir Isumbras's othodoxy :

> I shall never Hethen hounde become,
> Nor warre againste Christendome,
> Therfore to dye thys daye (he was willing).
> Greate wayes we have to gone,
> Meat ne drynke have we none,
> Ne penye for to paye.
> Syr, helpe us to our lyves fode,[1]
> For hys love that dyed on rode,[2]
> And let us walk awaye.

But this was not to be, for the Soudan was struck by the angelic beauty of the lady, and, after his Oriental manner, he wished to purchase her of her husband, offering him "an hundred pounde of fayre Florence rede and rounde, and red robes seven :" besides which, she was to

---

[1] Food.   [2] Rood, or cross.

be made the Soudan's queen. Needless to say, Sir Isumbras indignantly refused such a bargain, but the Soudan had *force majeure* on his side, paid the money and garments, and seized the lady. Sir Isumbras threw away the money, and, for his pains, got a terrible beating, from which, as soon as he was recovered, he took his son by the hand and went forth. Seemingly both Sir Isumbras and his wife looked upon these events as manifestations of the Divine will, and accepted them with resignation, for the Soudan immediately crowned the lady as his queen, and she made no resistance thereto, only stipulating to have a few last words with her former husband.

This was granted, and, after an affecting interview, she advised Sir Isumbras to go away, and, for the future, to exert all his energies in endeavouring to conquer and kill the Soudan, and enjoy his kingdom.

> Then this ladye meke and mylde
> Kyssed hym, and than her chylde,
> Then sowned [1] she tymes thre.

After which she sailed for Syria, and her husband, accepting the position, took the gold and red robes, and with his little son went on his way. At night, weary and tired, they lay upon the bare earth, but with the morn came an adventure, for an eagle carried off the red robes in which were wrapped both the gold, for which he had sold his wife, and also his provisions. He followed the

[1] Swooned.

bird till stopped by the shores of the Grecian Sea, over which the eagle flew, and he returned sadly to his young son, who, however, in the meantime, had been carried off by an unicorn; and this last blow utterly crushed the knight.

> The knyghte afore was often wo,
> But never then he was so,
> He set hym on a stone.
> Lorde, he saye, wo is me,
> For my wyfe and my chyldren thre,
> Now am I left alone.
> The kynge that bare of thorne the croune,
> Wysshe me a waye unto the towne,
> For all amysse have I gone.

Hungry, tired, and heartsore, he proceeded on his way, until he saw the light of a fire, which proceeded from a smith's forge. He begged for bread, but the smiths were utilitarian in their ideas, and refused to give any unless he worked for it. " They sayde, labour, for so do we." Sir Isumbras complied, and worked for them for a twelve-month in doing arduous and menial work, but after that time he was initiated into the art and mystery of working in iron, and he worked at this trade for seven years, becoming so proficient therein that he was enabled to make himself a suit of armour, and all that belonged to a knight's outfit.

At the end of that time he heard that the Christians had taken the field against the Saracens, and he determined to join them ; so, buckling on his armour, he got the best substitute for a charger that he could, "a croked caple that coles broughte," and started for the fray. Needless to say he fought like a paladin, until the poor " caple" was slain.   His prowess had been so prominent, that when this event happened, an Earl gave him a good steed and a fine suit of armour instead of his home-made one.   Thus accoutred, he once more mixed in the *mêlée*, dealing hard blows all round, and at last he slew the Soudan.   Such a feat as this could not fail of recognition by the Christian king, and Sir Isumbras was brought before him, all wounded as he was, and questioned as to who he was.

> Syr, quod he, a smythe's man,
> To defend thee in fyghte.

The king promised to make him a knight, and generally to look after his fortune, and, in the meantime, ordered him to a nunnery, where the good sisters might heal him of his wounds.   Here he was greatly petted,

> Because he had the Sowdan slayne,
> With many a Heathen hounde.

When he got well, he would not wait for honours to be bestowed upon him, but dressed himself like a palmer, and, having taken a grateful farewell of the prioress and the nuns, he again set out on his pilgrimage.   He found a ship sailing for Acre, and soon reached that city, from whence he prosecuted his pilgrimage to the Holy Sepulchre.   Hard and toilsome was the way, and the food,

too, poor and insufficient ; but a blessed change was at
hand, and he was about to reap the reward of his suffer-
ings.

> Faint and hungry,
> Beside the borowe [1] of Bethlem,
> He set hym by a well streme,
> Tyll the day was dymme.
> As he sat and sore syght
> There came an aungell about mydnight
> And brought hym bread and wyne.
> Isenbras, he sayde, lysten unto mee,
> Our lorde hath pardon graunted to thee,
> Forgeven are synnes thyne.
> Nowe rest the well, syr Isenbras,
> Forgeven is all thy trespas,
> Shortly for to sayne.[2]
> My Lorde is heaven['s] kynge
> Hath the geven hys blessynge,
> And byddeth the turne agayne.
> The knyght on his knees hym set,
> And Christ of heaven kynge he grete[d],
> Of the tydynges he was fayne.[3]

The angel left him, and Sir Isumbras, fortified by the
food he had taken, retraced his steps. He wandered
about until he heard of a fair castle, wherein dwelt a
queen, who was a paragon of all that was good, and

> Every day she made a dole
> Of many florences, gold and hole,[4]
> Whoso woulde it fetche.

Sir Isumbras was in that lowly condition when either

[1] Burgh, or town.   [2] Say.   [3] Glad.
[4] *I.e.*, not clipped, but nice and round, fresh from the mint.

money or meat would be acceptable, and at once made
for that castle.   He joined the ranks of the poor, and duly
received his golden florin from the queen, who chose
fifty of the poorest and feeblest from among them, and
Sir Isumbras with them.   The queen presided at the
feast of these poor folk, and, from some cause unexplained,
either from his superior state of emaciation, or from his
palmer's garb, denoting a pilgrimage to the Holy Land,
the steward gave directions that he should sit above all
the other company.   Food and drink were given him, but
he did not partake of them, but sat still, shedding tears.
Probably this behaviour called particular attention to him,
for the queen ordered a chair and a cushion to be provided for the poor palmer, that he might relate to her the
adventures he had met with in the many lands through
which he had travelled.   He gratified her curiosity with
many traveller's tales, but no temptation in the form of
rich meats, &c., could induce him to eat.   The queen bade
him dread nothing, but—

> For his soule that was my Lorde
> I will the finde at bed and borde,
> Fayre to cloth and feede.
> At thyne ease thou shalt be,
> With much mirth game and gle,
> Both early and late.
> A clene chamber and a fayre,
> And a man to serve thee
> Within the castle gate—

a position which was gratefully accepted by Sir Isumbras

who fell on his knees and thanked the queen ; but this promotion naturally brought with it envy from those less fortunate. At length there was a tournament, and he was horsed "on a fayre stede." His generous diet had brought back his old strength, and he played havoc with the Saracens ; none could stand before him.

> Some he caste over the lake,
> Of some both necke and backe he brake,
> They fled from hym for drede.
> The ladye seying that, fast lough,[1]
> And sayde my palmer is strong ynough,
> And worthy for to ryde.

And now a curious adventure befel Sir Isumbras, bordering somewhat on the marvellous : for, as he was walking one day, he espied a heron's nest, wherefrom fluttered a red cloth. Being somewhat amazed at this singular sight he climbed the tree, and in the nest he found his own red robe, of which the eagle had robbed him, still containing the gold which had been given him as the price of his wife, the sight of which well-nigh sent him mad.

> When he se the reade golde
> Wherfore hys ladye was solde,
> Then was he woode[2] of mynde.
> The golde into the chambre he bare,
> Under his heade he putte it there,
> Then wepynge he went his waye.
> Ever when he the golde gan se,
> Hys songe was well a waye.

[1] Laughed loudly.   [2] Mad.

Were he never of chere so good
Whan he in hys chamber yode [1]
After he wepte all the daye.

This lachrymose behaviour naturally attracted attention,
and was reported to the queen; and, by way of solving the
mystery, four knights broke open the door of Sir Isumbras' chamber, and found the red robes and the gold, which
they took to the queen, who, at the sight of these tokens,
especially of the gold for which she had been sold into
splendid slavery, swooned thrice.   When she came to
herself—

Often she syghed, and sayde alas,
This ought a knyght Syr Isenbras
That my lorde was wont to be.
Unto the knyghts there she tolde
How that she for golde was solde,
Her lorde was beaten there.
Where ye maye the palmer se
 Byd hym come and speke with me:
Therto me longeth sore.
The palmer came into the hall,
Unto counsell she dyd him call,
And asked hym right there.
How that he the golde wan,
And whether he were a gentleman,
And in what countre he was borne.
With carfull harte,[2] and rewfull [3] dreare
He gave the quene this aunswere
On knees her before.
The first tale that he her tolde
Madame therfore my wife was solde
I do you to understande.

[1] Went.   [2] Heart full of care.   [3] Rueful.

Thre chyldren have I lore,[1]
My mantel was awaye bore,
I in a nest it founde.
Tho[2] had the lady great solace,
She fell in sowning, so faynt she was
When they together met.
There was myrthe to se them mete
With clypping[3] and kissing swete
In armes for to folde.
Eyther of other was so fayne
They wolde it no longer layne ;[4]
To the knyghtes they it tolde.
A ryche brydale dyd they byd,
Both riche and poore thyther yede,[5]
Would none themselfe with holde.
Syr Isenbras was rayed[6] ryght,
And crowned kyng, that erre[7] was knyght,
With a gaye garlande of golde.

The chronicle does not treat of the happiness of the reunited pair, but it can well be imagined. It was hardly to be expected that his most Christian Majesty King Isumbras would live in friendly accord with the dogs of Mahound, his heathen neighbours ; nor, indeed, does he seem to have gained the affection of his own subjects, for when his neighbours rose against him, all his people, without exception, forsook him, and left him perfectly alone to fight the Saracen hosts.

Sir Isumbras does not seem to have quailed, although he felt he must be going to certain destruction. His parting from his queen is well told.

[1] Lost.   [2] Then.   [3] Embracing.
[4] They would no longer delay their reunion.
[5] Went.   [6] Arrayed, apparelled.   [7] Erst, before.

Syr Isenbras curtoyse and kene[1]
Toke hys leave of his quene,
And after syghed full sore.
He loked on her with eyen graye
And sayd, Madame, have good daye
For now and evermore.
The ladye sayd unto the knight,
I woulde I were in armure bright
With you that I myght fare.
If God woulde the grace sende,
That we myght together wende,
Then gone were all my care.
Sone was the lady dyghte[2]
In armure as she were a knyghte,
With horse, with speare, and shelde.
Agaynst thyrty thousand Sarasins, and mo
Of christen came but they two
Alone into the feylde.

Strong indeed must have been the faith that impelled
the pair to encounter the Saracenic horde. The heathen
raged furiously around them, but the knight was calm, and
swore by " swete Jesu " that he would not give in whilst
he " may in styrope stande," and his lady, following his
example, swore by " Mary mylde " that " she woulde do her
myghte." The battle began, and they twain did prodigies
of valour, overcoming all who came against them, until
the Soudan of the Saracens " was out of his wyt," and
promised rewards and lands to any one who would lay
Sir Isumbras low.

It was not to be done single-handed, and it was therefore proposed that a combined rush should be made on

---

[1] Earnest, bold.   [2] Clad.

Sir Isumbras, and thus overwhelm him with sheer force of numbers. This was done, and the knight and his lady were in such sore straits, that but a short time could only elapse before they certainly must be slain, when a miracle came to their aid.

> Ryght as they slayne shoulde have be,[1]
> There came ryding kynges thre
> On beastes that were wylde.
> One on a Leoparde, and one on a Unicorne,
> And one a Lion, one ranne beforne,[2]
> Theyr eldest sonne to beare.
> The knyghtes fought as they were wode,[3]
> And slewe all that before them stode ;
> Great wonder it was to se.
> The Heathen knyghtes slew the [4] there,
> The Sarasyns that counted were
> Thurtye thousand and thre.

It is needless to say that these three champions who arrived so opportunely were the three lost children of Sir Isumbras and his wife. The chronicle does not attempt to account for their sudden appearance other than " The grace of God us hether sent." Sir Isumbras' faithless subjects seem to have returned to their allegiance, and everything went very happily. The three sons each conquered him a " land," and christianized the people, and the Romance concludes.

> Than was Kynge Syr Isenbras
> Of more welth than ever he was,
> And come out of his care.

[1] Been.   [2] Before.   [3] Mad.   [4] They.

To every sonne he gave a lande,
And crouned hym kynge with his hande,
Whyle they together were.
The eldest sonne was in Surrye [1]
Chosen chyefe of chyvalre,
As kynge and governoure.
The seconde sonne, shortly to say,
In an Ile called Iaffaye
Reygned with great honour.
The youngest brother was crowned kynge
Of Calabre without leasynge : [2]
Thus reygned they all thre.
And when it pleased God of hys myght,
They all departed in heavens lyght,
To the whiche brynge us the trinitie,
Amen, Amen, for charitie.

[1] Syria.   [2] Lying.

Syr Degore

Sir Degore.

AS far as I can find, there is no MS. edition of this Romance in the British Museum, but it exists in the Auchinleck MSS., and there is another at Cambridge. The copy from which I have drawn was printed by Copland, circa 1550, and is one of the Garrick Collection in the British Museum. There was also a copy of this Romance printed by Wynkyn de Worde, 4°, 18 leaves with woodcuts, and another printed by John King, 1560, is in the Bodleian Library.

Once upon a time there was a king of England, whose name has not been handed down to us, who was very valiant, and highly skilled in martial exercises, and who loved nothing more than jousting. He had but one daughter, whose mother had died in giving birth to her, and he loved her dearly. Kings' sons and the great ones of the earth had wooed this princess, but hitherto without

success, because the king exacted from each suitor that
they should joust together, and only he who could lift the
king out of his saddle and both stirrups should wed her.
All had failed, and matters stood thus at the beginning of
the story.

It was his custom to celebrate the anniversary of his
queen's death with some solemnity in the abbey in which
she was buried, and this Romance commences with the
procession thither, in which the princess rode with her
father; but something happening amiss to her apparel, she
called her chamberlain and ladies-in-waiting to her, and
dismounted in order to put it right. This seems to have
taken some time, for when they started again the procession was both out of sight and hearing, and somehow they
took the wrong turning, and missed their way, getting lost
in a forest. It was very hot, they were tired, and they lay
down on the grass to rest, whilst the king's daughter went
and gathered flowers. She strayed so far that she lost her
companions, and, after the manner of her sex, she wept and
wrung her hands, fearing to be hurt by wild beasts.

Suddenly she saw before her a knight, richly dressed,
who begged her not to be afraid of him, for that he had
loved her many years, and that now, having met her thus
opportunely, he should gratify his passion. Utterly
paralyzed with fear and grief, she made no defence, and
before the knight left her, he gave her a present for the
son she should bear.

Therfore my swearde he shall have,
My good swerde of Ameaunt,[1]
For therwith I slewe a Gyaunt.
I brake the poynt in his head,
And in the felde I it leved ;
Dame, take it up, lo, it is here,
For thou spekest not with me this many a yere,
And yet peraventure tyme may come
That I may speke with my sonne,
And by this sworde I maye him ken.

Thus saying, he kissed and left her, and she, dazed and weeping, wandered about, carrying the sword, until she met with her retinue. Concealing the sword in her robe, she awoke them, and they once more went on their way, this time meeting many a knight spurring in hot haste, sent by the king in quest of them, and they proceeded to the abbey to attend the memorial service to her mother.

Time went on, and she could no longer conceal her position from herself, and, not knowing what to do, she took one of her maidens into her confidence, and told her all her history. With her connivance, the princess's son was born without any one else being the wiser, and the next thing was, how to get rid of the child. The maid wrapped it well in clothes, laid it in a cradle, and with it placed twenty pounds in gold and ten in silver, also

She put with him a payre of gloves,
Her leman gave her them in a stonde,[2]
They wold els on no womans hande,
On childes neither womans they nolde,[3]
But on his mothers handes they wolde,

[1] ? Adamant.   [2] Hurriedly.   [3] Would not (go).

And bad the chylde no wyfe wed in lande,
But the gloves wolde on her hande.
For they might serve no where,
Save the mother that dyd hym beare.
A letter with the chylde put she,
With the gloves also perde;[1]
She knyt the letter with a threde,
About his necke a full good spede,
Then was in the letter wrytte,
Whoso it founde shulde it wytte,[2]
For Christes love if anye good man,
This wofull chylde fynde can,
Do him[3] be christened of priestes hande,
And to helpe hym to lyve in lande,
With this sylver that is here,
Tyll he may armes bere,
And helpe hym with his owne good,
For he is come of gentyll bloud.

And, having thus carefully fitted out the infant for a foundling's career, she waited until the evening, and then stole out, she knew not whither, with the child.

Through thicke and thyn in the brere,[4]
She went all the wynter nyght,
By shyning of the mone light.

At length she reached a hermitage, and seeing the advantage of providing the solitary with a companion, she laid the cradle at the door, and hied back home. In the morning the hermit found the babe, and

He lyft up the shete anone,
And loked upon the lytel grome,[5]
Than helde up his ryght honde,
And thanked Jesus Christ of his fonde.[6]

[1] Par dieu, or par dé.   [2] Know.   [3] Let him, &c.
[4] Briar, tangled underwood.   [5] Man.   [6] Kindness.

He bare the childe into the chapel,
For joye of him he ronge the bel.
And layed up the gloves and the treasure,
And christened the childe with great honour,
And in the worshipe of the Trinite.
He called the childes name Degoré,[1]
For degore to understande it is
But thynge that almost lost iwys,
As thinge that almost ago,
Therfore he called that chylde so.

But whatever might be the holy man's joy, he found
he had got something beyond his power to cope with ; so
he sent Degoré to a married sister of his, and she and her
husband looked upon him as if he had been their own, and
kept him for ten years, by which time he had grown a
comely lad, well taught, and of a kindly disposition ; so
that nothing was left to be desired. He was then too old
for apron strings, so they sent him back to the hermit, who
" taught the childe of clerkes lore " for another ten years.

He was now twenty years old, tall, well built, and very
strong ; in fact, especially so for his years. So that when
the hermit found him fitted physically, by his strength, and
mentally, by his learning, for the battle of life, he looked
up the money, gloves, and letter that had accompanied
the babe, and, having deducted the ten pounds in silver for
his support and education, he gave him the remainder.
Naturally the young man burned to find his father, and

[1] In a MS. copy of this Romance it is spelt Degaré, which probably may
mean the modern *l'egaré*—led astray, or lost—which will reconcile it with the
text.

would not be contented except that he set out on his quest at once. So, taking only half his gold, he left the other in the charge of the good hermit, who advised him to buy a good horse and armour. But the youth would only take a "batte," or club, made of a good oak sapling, with which he could beat to the ground a good man well armed.

In those days an idle man in search of a job in the adventure line was never long without meeting with one. So on his first day, in the afternoon, whilst journeying through a forest, he heard the sound of mighty strokes. Going to the place whence they proceeded—

> There was an Erle both stout and gaye,
> He was come theyther the same daye
> For to hunt a dere or a do,
> But his houndes were gone hym fro.
> Then was there a Dragon great and grymme,
> Full of fyre and also venymme,
> Wyth a wyde throte and tuskes greate,
> Upon that knight faste gan he bete ;
> And as a Lyon then was hys feete,
> His tayle was longe and full unmete ; [1]
> Between hys head and his tayle
> Was ɤɤíí fote withouten fayle ;
> His body was lyke a wyne tonne,
> He shone full bryght agaynste the sonne ;
> His eyen were bright as any glasse,
> His scales were harde as any brasse,
> And therto he was necked lyke a horse ;
> He bare his head up with great force ;
> The breth of his mouth that dyd out blowe
> As it had bene a fyre on lowe ; [2]
> He was to loke on as I you tell
> As it had bene a fiende of hell.

[1] Unmeasured.   [2] Burning brightly.

The earl was getting weary of the strife, and prayed Degoré's help for the sake of "saynt charite." It was willingly accorded ; and, as the dragon began to feel on his ribs the effects of an oak sapling, skilfully and strongly applied, he turned his attention to the quarter whence the annoyance proceeded. The dragon was pounded and bruised, but, as dragons will not submit to such treatment with meekness, it used its tail with such effect that he knocked Degoré down. Quickly recovering, he redoubled his attentions to the dragon, and, having reduced its ribs to a jelly, and broken its legs, he finished up by dashing its brains out.

Very grateful was the earl for the timely succour, and he made Degoré accompany him to his palace, where, in addition to hospitable treatment, he dubbed him a knight, and fain would have given him " rentes, treasure, and halfe his lande." But Degoré would have none of them ; he only asked that the ladies of the establishment might be summoned and try on his gloves : if they fitted one of them, he would stay ; if not, he would take his leave. We who are behind the scenes know the result—they would fit no one ; but the earl would not let Degoré go away empty, so gave him a good steed and a suit of armour, a page, and a hackney for him to ride.

Thankfully he accepted these presents, and joyfully went on his way, which led him towards his grandfather's dominions.

Seeing many people, he stopped an esquire and asked him the reason for this assemblage. He was told that the king was holding a joust, the prize of which was to be his daughter's hand, if any knight could lift the king out of his saddle and both stirrups. The esquire detailed very graphically the fate of the competitors.

> For every man that rydeth to hym
> He beteth them with strokes grym;
> Some he breaketh the necke anone,
> Of some he cracketh both backe and bone,
> Some through the body he glytte,[1]
> And some to death he smytte.

But to a young man who at the very outset of his career had slain a dragon, this description would hardly act as a deterrent. He knew himself to be very strong, and he argued thus:

> I am in my yonge bloud,
> And I have horse and armure good,
> And, as I trowe, a full good steede,
> I will assaye if I maye spede,
> And I maye beare the kinge downe,
> I maye be a man of great renowne.

Thus revolving in his mind, he sought an inn, where he rested and enjoyed himself; until one day he met the king, and, kneeling before him, he told him that his lord had sent him to warn his Majesty that he was coming to joust with him; and the king made answer that any one coming on that errand was welcome.

[1] Literally, glides, slips through.

Be he knyght or barowne,
Erle, duke, or churle in towne.

The jousts were fixed for the morrow, and Degoré, fancy-
ing that he had by no means an easy task, and probably
being influenced by his education, went to church and
heard a mass to the Trinity, making an offering of a
florin to each of the three persons, the priest specially
praying for him. Then he went to his inn, armed himself,
bestrode his good steed, and took his lance, his squire following with another; and when he arrived at the place of tourney
he was the admired of all beholders, who had never seen
so fair a knight come on such an errand.

The joust began, and the king having the longer spear,
struck Degoré full on the shield; but, to his astonishment,
his adversary sat fast and safe in his saddle. At this the
king knew he had somebody out of the common way to
deal with, and, taking a yet longer spear at the next
assault, struck Degoré full on the breast, so that his horse
reared on high, and he was nearly thrown; but he rode out
his course. This fired Degoré's blood; twice had he been
smitten, and yet he had not touched the king; next time
he must do better, and once more the destriers charged,
and a splendid joust ensued. Fair on each other's shield,
were the lances planted, but the impetus was so great that
both were shattered and splintered.

And then the kynge began to speake,
Gyve me a speare that wyll not breke,

For he shall anone be smitten downe,
Though he be as stronge as Sampsone ;
And if he be the Devyll of hell
I shall him soone downe fell.

But this time the king's cunning forsook him, whilst Sir Degoré's lance hit him fairly. Alas! both horse and rider were rolling in the lists, the royal conditions being fairly fulfilled.

Great commotion followed the king's overthrow, and even the fair prize trembled as she thought she must now be married, and to a knight from a strange country, whose very name was unknown. The king held to his royal word, and greeted his conqueror kindly, saying that if his birth conformed to his appearance and deeds, he should think him a fitting successor to his land; meanwhile he gave him his daughter, and yielded to him his realm. Then and there was the marriage ceremony performed, and so it came to pass that Degoré married (unwittingly to both parties) his MOTHER.

Great feasting ensued, and night was drawing nigh when Sir Degoré bethought him that he ought never to wed any woman until she had tried on the magic gloves, and in the heaviness of his heart wished aloud that he had never been born, and that he were well out of the place. The king inquired why, and then Degoré told him how that he had done wrong in marrying without first subjecting his bride to a trial of his gloves.

And when the Lady gan this here
Anone she chaunged all her chere,
And all together tourned her mode ;
Her vysage waxed red as any bloude,
She knewe that the Gloves longed to her,
And sayd, geve me the Gloves, fayre Syr.
She toke the Gloves in that slede,
And lyghtly upon her handes them did ;
She fell downe and began to crye,
And sayd, Lorde God, I aske mercy ;
I am thy mother that dyd thee bere,
And thou arte myne owne sonne dere.

There was no questioning the truth of the assertion ; mother and son were locked in each other's arms, fondly kissing and embracing. The king looked on astonished, and naturally asked his daughter for an explanation, which she gave fully and unreservedly. Sir Degoré asked his mother if she knew of his father's whereabouts, but she had never seen him since their one fatal meeting ; but she gave Degoré the sole token she had of him, the pointless sword he had given her, together with his message that she was to keep it for their son, until the time that he had grown to man's estate. Sir Degoré eyed the blade critically, saying that he who had owned it must have been *a man ;* but he registered a vow that he would neither sleep night nor day until he had found his father, if that he were in Christendom.

So the next morning, after hearing mass, he set forth on his quest, attended only by his page—for he refused his grandfather's offer of some knights to accompany him—not knowing whither he was going, only ever riding westward, until he came to a forest and it was nigh nightfall. The sun was down, and no town was near, when the knight espied a castle, to which he sent his page to ask a night's lodging "for charyte." On this, the drawbridge fell, the gate stood open, and they entered. Like good cavaliers, their first thoughts were for their horses, and, finding plenty of corn and hay, they left them comfortable. They then went in search of human beings, but, although they roamed about and called out, they found none ; but in the midst of the hall was a great fire. This looked, undoubtedly, as if the castle were inhabited, and, determining to wait until some one should come, Sir Degoré sat himself on the daïs, and made himself comfortable.

His patience was rewarded, for a lady and three maidens appeared, dressed as Diana for the chase—

> . . . fayre and free,
> That were trussed up to the kne.

Two had bows, and two bore venison, and Sir Degoré courteously stood up and blessed them ; but they took no heed, and spoke not to him, but entered into a chamber, shutting the door after them. Soon after, however, came into the hall a dwarf, four feet high, who had a large head, with yellow hair, and a milk-white face. He was dressed in a green surcoat, edged with black and white fur, and was well clad, his shoes being fashionably turned up at the toes. Sir Degoré bowed courteously to him, yet the dwarf spoke no word, but began to furnish the board with a cloth and bread and wine. He lit torches in the hall, and made all things ready for supper.

Shortly afterwards there came from her bower a lady accompanied by fifteen damsels, some in red, and some in green. None of them took any heed of Sir Degoré, but went and washed their hands, and then sat down to supper —the lady on the daïs, five maidens on each side the table and five at the bottom. Sir Degoré was determined to make them speak if he could, so he went and sat before the lady, and commenced to eat ; but little food passed his lips, as he was so entranced by the beauty of the lady. Supper over, the dwarf brought water ; they all washed their hands, and left the hall for their private apartments. But Degoré could not stay after they had gone. He followed the lady, being determined to gaze his fill upon her lovely countenance, and found her sitting upon her bed, playing the harp. Sir Degoré sat him down and listened to the delicious music, which had such an effect upon him that he laid down and fell asleep, the lady kindly covering him ere she went to some other bed-chamber.

In the morning she came and called him, twitting him with his heavy slumber, and his discourtesy in going to sleep, instead of enjoying the company of herself and her maids. The knight begged forgiveness, and laid the blame

on the soft music, or else the good wine he had drunk ; and
then he naturally inquired about his host or hostess.

> But, tel me nowe, my Lady hende,
> Or I out of this chambre wende,
> Who hath this castel in his hande,
> And who is lorde of this lande ;
> Whether that ye be mayden or wyfe,
> And in what maner ye lede your lyfe,
> And why you have so many women
> Alone withoute any men ?

Her story was soon told : her father was a baron, who
owned the castle and town, she was his only child, and,
after his death, his heir. Many a knight had sought her in
marriage, but a hideous giant, whom it was impossible she
could love, was enamoured of her, and had disposed not
only of her suitors, by the simple process of killing them,
but also of all her men folk, save and except the dwarf who
had laid the supper. So saying, she fell down in a swoon.
Her damoiselles attended to her, and when she recovered
she gave Sir Degoré such a look, that he would have been
more than mortal, and less than knight, had he not answered
her that he would help her with all his power. Her gratitude
was such that she offered him herself and all her land in
case of victory.

Degoré was longing for the fight ; nor had he long to
wait, for the giant was approaching. Hastily he armed
and sallied forth. They met with so great a crash that
their spears were splintered, and Sir Degoré's horse having

been killed by the shock, he fell to the ground. He, however, was not hurt, for he sprang to his feet laughing, and drew his sword. The giant proved more courteous than the generality of his kind, and, scorning to be mounted whilst his adversary was on foot, he dismounted, in order that the combat might be fought on somewhat of an equality. It was continued with somewhat varied success, until Degoré smote such a blow that he shore the giant's helm and basinet, and divided his head. Even giants cannot survive such hurts, and this one gave up the ghost.

The lady, sitting in her castle, had seen the combat, and when

> Syr Degoré came to the castel,
> And against hym came that damesel,
> She thanked hym of his good deede,
> And to her chamber she dyd him leade ;
> She set hym on her bedde anone,
> And unarmed hym full sone ;
> She toke hym in her armes two,
> And kyssed hym a hundred tymes and mo,
> And sayde all my goods I wyll the geve,
> And my bodye while I lyve.

But Sir Degoré had to explain that he had set out with a fixed purpose, and that this giant-slaying was but an interlude. He had to go to a far country, but that at the end of twelve months he would return to her, and in the meantime he committed her to the keeping of the Almighty. The fair one wept at his departure, but he was inexorable and set out on his journey.

Long rode he, ever going westward, until in a forest he met a knight arrayed in superb armour, richly ornamented with gold and azure, bearing as his arms three boars' heads. He asked Sir Degoré what he was doing in his forest slaying his deer. Degoré denied the imputation, saying that he was an adventurous knight going to seek wars and fighting. The stranger knight evidently took this to mean an invitation to combat, and in that light it was at once accepted. With lances couched they met, but that of Sir Degoré being the longest, he smote the stranger knight full upon the shield, so that his lance splintered; but the knight sat fast in his saddle. Taking each a fresh lance, they once more met, and this time with such force that both their horses were killed.

Then they fought on foot; but ere long the stranger noticed that Sir Degoré's sword was pointless, and, calling out for a short truce, breathlessly asked where was he born, and in what land?

> Syr, he sayd, in England,
> A kynges doughter is my mother,
> But I wot not who is my father.
> What is thy name, then sayd he,
> Syr, my name is Degoré.
> Sir Degoré thou art welcome,
> For wel I wote thou art my sonne;
> By this swerde I know the here;
> The point is in my pautenere.[1]
> He took the poynt and sette it to,
> And they accorded bothe two.

[1] A purse, or pocket.

At this convincing proof of paternity, the father and son embraced, nothing doubting, and set out in company for England, which they reached in safety, and at once rode to the king's palace. Degoré's mother saw them coming.

> And when the ladye sawe that syght,
> She went to them with all her myght ;
> And ryght well she them knewe,
> And then she chaunged all her hewe,
> And sayd my dere sonne Degoré,
> Thou hast thy father brought with thee.

The strange knight owned to the fact. The king rejoiced in the truth of his daughter's story. She and the knight were married, and then Sir Degoré and his father set out to visit the lady, whom he had defended from the giant. They were wedded with great solemnity, and everybody, for ever after, was happy.

"Thus endeth the tretyse of Syr Degoré."

Sir Bevis of Hampton.

OF this Romance I can find no MS. in the British Museum, but it was an especial pet of the early Italian Printers, there being many editions in different Italian cities in the early sixteenth century, and one was printed as early as 1497 at Bologna. *Buovo de Antona de Guidone Palladius Rezunto et revisto. Caligula di Bazalieri.* Ebert quotes two early French editions, one—*Le livre de Beufoes de Hantonne et de la Belle Josienne sa mye. Par Verard.* But to this there is no date ; it was probably earlier than the *Beufues Danthonne nouvellement imprimé a Paris. Par le Noir.* 1502.

Of English copies, there is one in the Bodleian Library, printed by Pynson ; and Hazlitt says a fragment of two leaves, printed by Wynkyn de Worde, is in existence. The copy from which I have taken the Romance is printed by Copland, and the British Museum gives an approximate date of 1550.

M. Amaury Duval, in his *Histoire Litteraire de la*

France, vol. xviii. p. 749, tries to show that this Romance
was of French extraction, and that the Anton from which
Sir Bevis derived his name was Antonne, a town in
France.   But when we consider that the River Anton, or
Test, flows by Southampton, that there is a Bevois Mount
where he is supposed to be buried, and that the Bar Gate
is ornamented with paintings of both Bevis and Ascaparte,
we cannot yield our hero to the French.

Sir Bevis of Hampton had for father the famous Earl
of Southampton—Sir Guy, who, the chronicler informs us,
lived in the time of King Edgar.   When he was young,
Sir Guy was a very paladin, and his prowess was known
throughout the civilized world.

> In every land he rode and yede,[1]
> For to wynne him price and mede :[2]
> In Fraunce, in Flaunders, and in Almaine ;[3]
> In Brabant, in Cecele,[4] and in Britayne ;[5]
> In Denmarke, Calyce,[6] and in Gasconne ;
> In Hungary, Calabre,[7] and in Burgoyne ;
> In Pole, in Normandy, and in Mayne ;
> In Turkye, Nabrant,[8] and in Spayne ;
> In Eastland,[9] Norway, and in Picardye ;
> In Scotland, in Wales, and in Lumbardye ;
> In Christendome, and also in heathenesse,
> Full well is known Sir Guyes worthinesse.
> *   *   *   *   *   *
> Whyle he was younge and jolye,
> Wolde Syr Guy weed no wyfe ;
> But whan that he was olde,
> He waxed feble, croked and colde,
> Than toke he his leve of chevalry.

[1] Went.   [2] Prize and reward.   [3] Germany.   [4] Sicily.   [5] Brittany.
[6] Calais.   [7] Calabria.   [8] Tartary.   [9] Muscovy, or Russia.

Then, for the first time in his life, he seems to have thought of matrimony, and his choice fell upon the daughter of the King of Scotland, who was not only much younger than he, but was in love with Sir Murdure, the brother of the Emperor of Almaine. However, in those days, young ladies had to obey the will of their parents. So these two made a *mariage de convenance*, and the fruit of their union was Sir Bevis.

But, as time went on, and Bevis grew into boyhood, the difference of age between the married couple became more apparent ; Sir Guy, his wife complained, "All day he hideth in the churche," and she longed for the more ardent companionship of her young lover. The perpetual brooding on her wasted life first tempted her, and then led her, into sin. She procured a pliant and trusty messenger, and gave him the following instructions :

> Go, she sayde, to Almayne,
> And grete well fro me Syr Murdure,
> Brother to the Emperoure,
> And byd him in the fyrst daye
> Of the moneth of Maye,
> That he in the foreste be,
> Well armed with his meine ; [1]
> Byd him that it be not lened,[2]
> But that my lorde be there heded ; [3]
> And sende it me to [4] a present,
> My lorde shall naked [5] to him be sent.

This cruel message was duly delivered, and, on the appointed day, Sir Murdure and his men lay in ambush in

[1] Company.   [2] Behind hand.   [3] Beheaded.   [4] As.   [5] Unarmed.

the forest near Hampton. The wicked wife feigned sickness, which she declared could only be cured by eating
wild boar's flesh. Sir Guy immediately promised that he

SIR GUY TRAITOROUSLY SLAIN BY SIR MURDURE.

would procure some for her, and, accompanied by his
followers, unsuspectingly entered the wood, where he soon
encountered Sir Murdure.

This false knight made no scruple of openly telling Sir

Guy of the errand he had come on, and the old knight put himself on the defensive. He performed prodigies of valour. He wounded the traitorous Sir Murdure, and, with his own hands, killed a hundred of his foes ; but, alas! his horse was slain, and he was brought to the ground. The sad fate of the poor old man is graphically told.

> Than kneled Guy to Syr Murdure,
> And said marcy and succoure;
> And sayde Murdure for thy gentry,[1]
> Thus cowardly let me not dye.
> But lend me horse, armoure, and sheld,
> And let me dye here in the felde;
> And with thee that I do so,
> I thee forgyve and thou me slo ;[2]
> Than cried they all in this wyse,
> Sle [2] him that he never ryse.
> With that syr Murdure to hym yede,
> And smote there of his head.
> To a knight he toke his hede in hande,
> Go he sayd, and bare this fonde [3]
> To the countesse that is so bright,
> And say I come to her boure this night.

At this time Sir Bevis was but a child—seven years of age—but he appears to have had knowledge beyond his years, and, when he heard of the treacherous death of his father, and of his mother's shameless sin, he went to her, upbraided her with her conduct, and swore that, if he ever bore arms, he would avenge his father with might and main. His mother smote him to the ground, and com-

---

[1] An appeal to his birth and breeding. [2] Slew. [3] Token of affection.

manded his uncle (his father's brother), Sir Sabere, to slay him. Possibly it was policy on Sir Sabere's part to temporize with the dominant party, and he promised compliance. But instead of killing the boy, he victimized a pig, and, sprinkling Bevis's clothes with its blood, he showed them as evidence of his having done the behests of the wicked Countess. As to the young Bevis, he clothed him in mean attire, and set him to tend sheep, promising to send him to Wales, where dwelt an Earl, who was a relation, and who would train him to arms as soon as he was old enough to bear them, when he might avenge his father.

Whilst engaged in the lowly occupation of herdboy, he heard trumpets and tabors, and the sound of the festivities in which the sinful pair were indulging, and he could not control his indignation when he thought upon his father's death, and contrasted his own sad plight with that of the guilty ones. His wrath overcame his prudence, and he went straight to the castle, where the porter refused him admittance, but Bevis knocked his brains out, and went into the hall, where he addressed his mother, and Sir Murdure, in language more forcible than polite, and, finally, smote the evil knight so that he swooned. The knights, who were feasting, seemed to have sympathized with the boy, for they let him pass, and he went home to Sir Sabere, who was sorely puzzled what to do with him, and, as a temporary measure, hid him in a chamber.

Scarcely was he concealed, when the Countess arrived

in a furious state of mind, vowing that Sir Sabere should suffer for his nephew's conduct. Bevis, hearing this, came from his hiding-place, and confronted his unnatural mother. The sight of the boy seems to have roused her to ungovernable fury, and she commanded Sir Sabere, and another knight, to take him and cast him into the sea. This they promised to do, but compromised the matter, and salved their consciences by selling him to the Paynims, whose ships were at the sea shore for trading purposes. By them he was carried to the land of Armony, or Armenia, then governed by a king called Ermine, who had a daughter; and, as we shall hear a great deal of this lady in the course of the story, it will be as well to give her description, as the chronicler's exposition of his ideal of feminine perfection.

> He had a doughter fayre and bryght,
> Josian that fayre mayde hight ; [1]
> Her visage was whight as lylly floure,
> Therin ranne the rede coloure,
> With bright browes and eyes shene, [2]
> With heare as gold wire on the grene ;
> With comly nose and lyppes swete,
> With lovely mouth and fayre fete,
> With tethe white and even sette ;
> Her handes [3] were swete as vyolet,
> With gentill body withouten lacke,
> Well shapen both belly and backe ;
> With smale handes and fingers longe;
> Nothing of her was shapen wronge,
> Wherfore should I her not decyve,
> There was never none fayrer on lyve.

[1] Called. [2] Shining. [3] Breath.

The heathen merchants made Bevis a present to the king, who was much struck with his personal appearance and strength ; and, when the lad had told his story, and avowed his parentage, the king remembered Sir Guy, whose trenchant sword had laid low many a Paynim and Saracen.

> Bevis, he sayde, I have no heyre,
> But a doughter that is fayre ;
> And thou wylte thy lorde forsake,
> And to Apolyn [1] our god thee betake.
> I shall geve her to be thy wyfe,
> And all my lande after my lyfe.

But nothing could induce Bevis to change his religion ; so the king told him that, whilst he was young, he should be his chamberlain, and when old enough to be dubbed a knight, he should bear the king's banner in battle. And so Bevis was brought up an universal favourite, but looked upon by the fair Josian with eyes of love ; and by the time he was fourteen years old, he was the very paragon of a squire.

It was on a Christmas Day, and Bevis was riding with some sixty Saracens, when one laughingly asked him if he knew what day it was. He replied that he was but seven years old when he was sold into heathenesse, and they must not blame him if he failed in his knowledge of that particular day. They began jeering him, and he did not do much towards keeping the peace, by declaring that if

[1] Apollyon.

he were armed he would joust with them one after the
other. This seems to have been more than the Saracenic
temper could bear, and they all set upon him. Weapon-
less, he was soon wounded, but—

> Bevis was light and quicke,
> And to the Sarasyn gan he lepe,[1]
> And with his fyste he stroke faste
> That his cheke bone all to braste.[2]

Possessing himself of a Saracen's sword, he smote all
before him, in spite of all their endeavours—indeed, he
seems to have borne a charmed life ; and, for a boy of fourteen, he performed prodigies of valour.

> Aboute Bevis the Sarasyns dyd lepe,
> As they had bene a flocke of shepe,
> Of some he gan ye woundes down tere [3]
> That the guttes trayled here and there.
> There was no Sarason that he hette [4]
> But his body asonder he kette ; [5]
> There myght none fle by no syde,
> But Bevis made him to abyde ;
> And Bevis within a litle stounde [6]
> The .lx. Sarsons had brought to grounde.

The horses of the slaughtered Saracens fled home ;
Bevis followed them, and, having stabled his horse, he
went into his chamber and sunk upon the floor, faint with
his wounds and loss of blood. King Ermine was very
wroth at the loss of his sixty Saracens, and swore he
would eat no bread until Bevis were dead ; but Josian

---

[1] He sprang.   [2] Smashed.   [3] *I.e.*, made long slashes.
[4] Hit.   [5] Cut.   [6] While.

pleaded for her love, and suggested that first of all Bevis's
story should be heard.   The king agreed, and Josian sent
two knights to ask Bevis to speak with her ; but, whether it
was from the pain of the wounds, or that his blood had
not yet cooled after his arduous exertions, he returned the
very uncourteous message : " I wyll not ones styre of this
grounde, to speake with any heathen hounde," and then he
gave a more particular message to the two knights, after
which they incontinently fled.

> Unchristened houndes, I rede you, fle,
> Or I your herte blode shall se.

They reported Bevis's intractable state of mind to
Josian, who bade them come with her and fear not ; and,
when they reached Bevis's chamber, she kissed him and
raised him up, and, promising to cure him of his wounds,
led him to the king, her father, who, when he saw Bevis's
thirty wounds, and heard his version of the story, his " teres
ranne downe plenty," and he ordered Josian to exercise
her leech craft on the patient, and heal his wounds, if
possible : a task she willingly undertook, and what with
salves and drinks, and a great deal of kissing, Bevis was
soon made whole.

In King Ermine's forest was a fierce wild boar, whose
tusks were the dread of all men, and the creature was of
abnormal size.   Bevis, having got sound and strong again,
bethought him of this boar, and could not rest contented
until he had tried conclusions with it.   So, early one

morning, he armed himself, and, getting on horseback, set off on his adventure, to the great admiration of Josian, who watched him from a window. When he came to the wood he tied up his horse and went in search of the boar, blowing his horn as he went on his way ; but the boar heeded not the horn blowing, and Bevis had to be guided to its den by the bones of men which the fell beast had slain.

When visible, it was not a pleasant animal to look at, and, when attacked, proved quite capable of taking care of itself. Bevis's boar spear was snapped into seven parts at the onset, and, when the champion laid on him with his sword, it had no effect.

> Bevis thought at eche dynt [1]
> That he had smiten upon a flinte.

And so the battle waged till it was noon, when Bevis was so weary he thought he should die. The boar, too, had had enough of it, and was faint and feeble, so that it turned to the plain, whither Bevis followed it, and, as the boar came towards him, open-mouthed, he thrust his sword down its throat, and "clove his herte asonder," and, cutting off the head of his grisly foe, he stuck it on the truncheon, or broken part of his boar spear.

The regular foresters had hitherto been afraid to cope with this awful beast, but when they saw him slain by Bevis they were filled with envy and hatred, and con-

[1] Stroke.

spired together to slay him and possess themselves of the
boar's head. They were twelve in number, and all well
armed, whilst Bevis had but the truncheon of his spear,

BEVIS FIGHTS THE FORESTERS.

for he had forgotten his sword after cutting off the boar's
head. The foresters set upon him, but, needless to say,
they got the worst of it. Nine of their number bit the

dust, never to rise again, whilst the other three fled from his wrath. Bevis remounted the boar's head, and went in triumph towards the royal residence ; the whole scene having been enacted before the eyes of the loving Josian. King Ermine, when the boar's head was presented to him, took the loss of his foresters in good part, admiring the prowess of Bevis.

In those days one adventure trod upon the heels of another.

> Sone after, not long during,
> Came a messenger to Ermine ye king
> For [1] Kynge Bradmounde of Damas,[2]
> That swore by Mahounde and Golyas,
> But [3] of King Ermine blive [4]
> Sende Josian to be his wyfe,
> In all waies he would him noie,[5]
> And all his land robbe and destroye,
> And sayde in the fyrst day of Maye
> He shoulde come and holde his daye,
> And send away his doughter then,
> And his landes destroye and brenne.

King Ermine was naturally wroth, and sent for his earls and barons, but Josian could not refrain from recommending Bevis, and told the king how valuable would be the assistance of his arm, if he were dubbed a knight, and thus enabled to take a prominent part in the defence of the kingdom. The king sent for Bevis, made him a knight, and gave him the chief command of his forces ; and his equipment, which is noteworthy, as it figures more than once in the story, is thus described :

[1] From. [2] Damascus. [3] Unless. [4] Quickly. [5] Annoy.

Bevis did on he auctowne [1]
That worthied [2] many a towne.
An hauberke Josian him brought,
A better hauberke was never wrought ;
A helmet she gave him good and faire,
There might no thing it appayre.[3]
Than gave him that fayre maye [4]
A good swerde that hight [5] Morglay,
There was no better under the sonn,
Mani a lande therwith was wonn.
Josian gave him suche a stede,
The best that ever on grounde yede ; [6]
Full well can I his name tell,
Men called him Arundell ;
No horse in the world was so strong
That might him sue [7] a forlonge.

Thus equipped, he sprung into the saddle, and sounded his horn, so that his followers might know the rallying sound. His force consisted of twenty thousand barons ; but King Bradmound had twice as many, and, when the opposing forces met, he laughed loudly at the small force sent against him. He had a gigantic standard bearer, King Radison, who passed for the champion of the army, and at him Sir Bevis went. A short passage of arms, and Radison lay dead, with Sir Bevis's spear right through him. Then, with Morglay, he killed a hundred Saracens, and, indeed, wherever he went, " heades trindle like a ball," the invincible sword working wonders. At last he en-

---

[1] Put on his haqueton, or quilted waistcoat, worn under the coat of mail.
[2] That was worth.   [3] Damage.   [4] Maid.
[5] Called ; all the famous swords of chivalry were named, as Arthur's Excalibur.   [6] Went.   [7] Follow, pursue.

countered Bradmound himself, and, after a brief combat, the foe was at his mercy. This Bradmound sought, offering castles and towers to his conqueror in exchange for his life. But Bevis had his own views on the subject, and would only grant the boon on condition that Bradmound became King Ermine's " man," or vassal.

> Bevis charged him in his laye
> That he shoulde never by night ne by daye
> Wayte Kinge Ermine with no treason,
> But ever be at his sommon,
> And hold him of thy lands as chefe.

Had Sir Bevis the gift of prescience, it would have been better, as the chronicler remarks, for him to have killed King Bradmound at once ; but he was content with his decisive victory, and returned to King Ermine, taking with him two captured knights as his guests.

> The King Ermine was glad and blithe,
> And blessed Bevis often sithe.

And he told Josian to unarm the hero, and to look after his personal welfare—a task which the maiden most gladly undertook, for her exceeding love towards him, and, indeed, she told him that she would rather have his naked body than anything that Mahound could give; but, finding him still cold to her advances, she upbraided him, calling him a churl, and bidding him go hence. He retired to his chamber, but Josian, left to herself, soon repented of her conduct to Sir Bevis, and sent her chamberlain,

Boniface, with a reconciliatory message, begging Sir
Bevis to come to her. This he would not do, as he said
she herself had bade him begone. Boniface returned and
told his lady, who, finding that Bevis would not come to
her, determined to go to him, and accordingly went to
his chamber, where she found him awake.

> Bevis, she sayde, a whyle awake,
> I am come my peas to make.
> Damoysell, sayde Bevis, then,
> Let me lye, and go me from.
> Mercy, she sayde, my lemman [1] swete,
> She fell downe and beganne to wepe,
> Forgyve me that I have mis-saide,
> I wyll that ye be well apayde, [2]
> My false gods I wyll forsake,
> And Christendome for thee to take.
> On that covenant sayd Bevis than
> I wyll the love, fayre Josyan.

This, then, was the strange wooing of Sir Bevis and
the fair Josian, who, in their after life, met with many
crosses, yet lost not faith in each other.

And now is introduced an episode of moral turpitude
it would be difficult to match. Bevis had treated the two
knights whom he had captured in his fight with Bradmound as his brothers, lodged them in his house, and
fed them at his table ; yet these two, by playing eavesdroppers, overheard the love passages of Bevis and Josian,
and immediately went, open-mouthed, to the king, to

---

[1] Love.   [2] Paid.

inform him of his daughter's apostacy. Their behaviour
is thus commented on in the metrical version:

> It is sothe by all hallowes [1]
> Delyver a thefe fro the gallows,
> He shall the wate [2] to robbe or slo ; [3]
> So it fared by the knightes two :
> Bevis delivered them from peryll,
> And they guytte him full yll.

King Ermine was exceeding wroth, not on account of
the love his daughter bore to Bevis, but because he was
a Christian, for whose sake Josian would deny her gods.
Yet he felt that it would not be politic to punish Bevis
openly, and one of his court suggested a plan of getting
rid of the hero without undue publicity. This was to
write a letter to Bradmound, charging him to seize Bevis
and keep him in durance, and get the unsuspecting knight
to be the bearer of the missive.

Bevis was sent for, and entrusted with the letter, being
strictly charged by the treacherous Ermine not to break
the seal or pry into its contents. He asked for his horse
Arundel and his sword Morglay, but the king negatived
the suggestion, pointing out that, as he was going on a
pacific errand, an easy hackney would be most befitting.
Not only did he go unarmed and without his good steed,
but he neglected his commissariat, so that after two or
three days' riding he suffered both from hunger and thirst,
which, added to his bodily weariness, overcame him, and

---

[1] The saints.   [2] Lie in wait.   [3] Slay.

he got down from his saddle and stretched himself on the ground to sleep, whilst his horse cropped the grass. When he awoke he saw a palmer near him, who had a bountiful feast spread before him of bread and wine and three baked curlews. The palmer recognized Sir Bevis's social position, and courteously invited him to share his meal, which he did. His hunger being appeased, he questioned the palmer as to who he was, and was told that his name was Terry, the son of Sir Sabere, who had sent him in quest of his nephew Bevis, with strict injunctions that he was to roam all over the world, but that he must find him, for Bevis was wanted to fight for his heritage against Sir Murdure. Bevis, for some reason, did not disclose himself, but professed to be the bosom friend of that knight, and said that he would give him the palmer's message as soon as he had accomplished the mission he had on hand. Then, having kissed each other, they went their several ways—the palmer towards England, Sir Bevis towards Damascus.

That city was duly reached, and the magnificence of Bradmound's palace excited Sir Bevis's admiration; but he met with no adventure until he came to some Saracens sacrificing to their idol Mahound. Fired with holy zeal, he overturned the idol in the mire, and the natural consequence ensued; for the Saracens resented this desecration, and fell upon the perpetrator of the sacrilege. Although Sir Bevis had left Morglay at home, and had but a common sword, he soon killed two hundred of his enemies, and the others fled to the palace, where they reported the slaughter to the king, who at once went to see into the affair. When Sir Bevis saw the king, he kneeled down and delivered his letter. This the king gave to a *clerk* to read, and when its contents had been mastered, the king rejoiced exceedingly, and began by upbraiding Sir Bevis with the deeds of valour he had done to Bradmound's detriment, and said he should be slain. Bevis implored that he might not die a dog's death, but rather that he should die fighting against any numbers, even sixty thousand men. But the revengeful Saracen had determined that he should " die with muche sorowe." One more struggle he made for liberty, and the souls of sixty Saracens were liberated, but he was overpowered by numbers, and bound.

They did him mock honour, seating him in hall, in a knight's stall, and fed him with choice meats and drinks, the king taunting him the while with the fact that this should be his last meal. He was then taken to a dungeon where he was left unbound. Searching about, he found a short truncheon, which weapon he speedily appropriated, and he also discovered that a stream of water ran through his prison.

He had been there but a little while, when two dragons made their appearance, with the intention of making a meal of Sir Bevis, but he encountered them bravely with

his truncheon, and slew them both after a combat which
lasted all that day and night, until the next noon—a fight
so severe that at its close but very little of the truncheon
was left in his hand.   His lot was a hard one.

> Seven winters he was thore,
> Meate he had never more
> But once a daye withouten messe [1]
> Of wheat bran he had a messe ;
> Brede or corne ete he none,
> But of water he had great wone ; [2]
> Rattes and myse and suche smal dere
> Was his meate that seven yere.

During this time how fared Josian ?   She soon missed
her lover, and straitly asked her father what had become
of him ; and he falsely answered that he had gone to live
on his estate in England, where he had married a king's
daughter.

> Than was Josian full of wo,
> And to her chamber she did go,
> And wept sore for Syr Bevis,
> And thought some treason here is ;
> There is no man can tell the sorowe
> That she made both even and morowe.

The loss of Sir Bevis was not her sole affliction.   She
was again sought in marriage ; this time by Joure, King of
Mambraunt, whose suit found favour in her father's eyes,
and she was commanded to marry him.   She durst not
disobey ; and they were married.   However, although
wedded, she was determined to preserve her chastity, and
to that purpose she had recourse to a charm.

[1] Without missing.   [2] Quantity.

I shall never so untrew be
As thou art, Bevis, to me :
I shall now go and make me a writte
Through a clarke wyse of witte,
There no man shall have grace
While the letters are in this place,
Against my wyll to lye me by,
Nor do me shame nor vylany.

This charm she hung around her neck, and it fully answered its purpose, for, after their espousal, they set out for King Ermine's court. The king, wishing to do his son-in-law all the honour in his power, met him on the way, and presented him with Arundel and Morglay. Struck by the beauty of the horse, King Joure mounted him to ride into the city ; but the horse, finding his rider was not Bevis, leaped over hedge and ditch, briar and corn, until he had thrown the unfortunate king and broken his back—of which hurt he died. Poor Arundel, as the cause of the mischief, was bound with great ropes, and had no food nor water given him ; and, had it not been through the kindness of Josian (now Queen of Mambraunt), who privily fed him, he would have been starved.

Bevis, meanwhile, was in evil case, rotting in a foul dungeon, with only carrion for food ; his person neglected, and his hair long and matted, yet was he not forsaken by the Almighty. The story goes that one night an adder bit him on his brow, and the pain having awakened him, he prayed to God for help ; and immediately an angel appeared and cured him. After this, his piety became more demonstrative, and his petitions were so fervid, that they were overheard by his two gaolers, who, because their prisoner so despised Mahound, thought it would be a meritorious deed to kill him. One of them, taking a cord and lanthorn, lowered himself into the dungeon, and smote Bevis so that he fell ; but, after a short prayer, he threw himself upon his gaoler, and, with his fists only, broke his neck. After a while the other warder descended, but, when he saw his fellow dead, he would have fain climbed up again ; but Sir Bevis prevented him, and killed him with the sword of gaoler No. 1.

The murder of his gaolers naturally deprived him of his " bran messe," and for three days he had no food. He had recourse again to prayer ; and, by a superhuman effort, he was enabled to reach the rope by which the warders had descended, and thus climb up to the level of the ground. This happened about midnight, and, listening, he heard

> . . . in the stable
> Gromes synge, and make bable.[1]

They were dressing the royal horses, and, as he stood in need of a good steed for his escape, he burst open the door, killed a few grooms, and chose the best horse for himself. He then woke the porter, by telling him that Bevis of Hampton had escaped, and that he was in pursuit. On this the gates were unlocked, and Bevis rejoiced once more in freedom. The poor janitor, on going his rounds, found

[1] Babble, talk.

the gaolers dead, and Sir Bevis missing, and thus woke up
to a sense of the situation, causing him to remark—

> . . . By my snoute
> That was Bevis that I let oute.

He at once reported the loss to the King Bradmound,
who lost but little time in fretting over it, but took prompt
measures, summoning his barons, and specially one, Sir
Graunders, who had a wonderful horse called Truncefyce,
said to be worth its weight in gold. Sir Graunders was
the first ready, and set off at once in pursuit, thinking to
win the prize easily ; and he soon came up with Sir Bevis.
The greetings usual in such cases were exchanged, and
then they fought. The combat was soon over.

> Bevis turned him well and fayre,
> And rode together with great ayre ;
> Suche a stroke him gave Graunder
> That through helme and halberke cler
> Hert and bodi he clave in sunder,
> There helped no armour, yt was wonder
> Ryght to the sadle be hed mine,
> And clove him downe as a swyne.

The next thing was to possess himself of the matchless
steed Truncefyce. The combat had, naturally, somewhat
delayed him, and, when he was mounted, he saw King
Bradmound and his host in hot pursuit. He fled on until
he came to the sea, in which he thought he would rather
perish than be slain by the heathen ; so, after a pious
ejaculation, he put the good horse at it and leaped forty
feet into the sea. This feat the Saracens dared not

emulate, and Truncefyce bore him safely to the opposite
shore; but so feeble was Bevis, that, when the horse
reached the land, and shook himself, the rider fell to the
ground. Such was his famished condition that he
remarked—

> Lorde, sayd Bevis, how hongry am I,
> And I were Kyng of Armony,
> I would in geve withouten reade
> For a shever [1] of browne breade.

He remounted his horse, and had not ridden long when he
came to a fair castle, on whose wall was a lady, whom the
famished knight conjured: "For his love that dyed on a
tre, one mele's mete thou geve me." But the lady begged
him to go away, explaining that her husband was a giant,
who believed in Mahound and Termagaunt, who would
take a pleasure in slaying a Christian. But Bevis insisting
that there, and there only, would he eat food, she was
obliged to go and tell her husband, who was Sir Graunders'
brother. He was naturally annoyed, especially when he
recognized Truncefyce; and he asked Bevis whence he
had stolen him. Sir Bevis replied, mockingly, that at their
last meeting he had shorn Sir Graunders' crown for him,
and made a deacon of him, but that he would make a
priest of the giant. This taunting could not be endured,
and the giant struck out at Bevis, missed him, but killed
Truncefyce, and the battle waged on foot. The giant sent

[1] Slice.

a dart through Bevis's shoulder, and he retorted by a blow which severed the giant's head from his body.

Then his appetite again asserted its sway, and he would have meat. The new-made widow durst not refuse the conqueror, and she served him with bread, wine, and fine meats, all of which, as a precautionary measure against poison, he insisted upon her tasting. Refreshed by this food, he bound up his wound, and, with a light heart, resumed his journey, only wishing that King Bradmound and his army were before him, that he might enjoy the pastime of slaughtering them.

So he rode on until he came to Jerusalem, where he took the opportunity (having lived so long in heathen lands) of confessing to the Patriarch, who gave him absolution, and kept him as his guest until he was quite cured of his wounds, and recovered from his fatigues. One thing the Patriarch especially charged him—

> And forbod him on his lyfe
> That never he should wedde a wyfe
> But if she were a mayden clene.

Taking leave of the Patriarch, he rode on, revolving in his mind what his future course of action should be, whether he should go to England and slay his stepfather, or go to the kingdom of Armony and look after the fair Josian. And, while he rode, thus self-communing, he met with a knight, an old comrade, and they went on their way together, the knight giving him news, to which, from his long imprisonment, he was a stranger. How that Josian had been married to King Joure of Mambraunt,[1] who was then owner both of Arundel and his sword Morglay.

This decided Sir Bevis, and he at once turned his steps towards Mambraunt, which, when he reached, he would not enter as a knight, but exchanged his horse with a palmer for his clothes. On his arrival at the palace, he found many pilgrims waiting, and, on being questioned, they informed him that every day the queen distributed alms for the love of Bevis of Hampton. Finding that this would not take place until the afternoon, he wandered round the palace, and heard, in a turret, Josian making moan for him.

He joined the pilgrims at the almsgiving, but was singled out by Josian, who asked him if in any land he had heard of Bevis of Hampton. Yes, he replied, he knew him well enough ; for they were both earls, and often had he heard him tell of his horse Arundel, and much would he like to see him. The queen led Bevis to the stables, when he went up to and spoke to Arundel, who no sooner heard the voice of his loved master than he burst seven chains that confined him, and ran out, neighing loudly. The queen was afraid that the horse would hurt some one, but Sir Bevis bade her fear nought, for he could manage him ; and, leaping on Arundel's back, the scales fell from Josian's

---

[1] The chronicler, here, has availed himself of poetic license; for, in a former part of the Romance, Aundel threw, and killed, King Joure immediately after his wedding with Josian.

eyes, and she recognized her old love. She at once reminded him of his promise to make her his wife if she forsook her false gods—told him that she would get him his good sword Morglay, and begged of him to take her with him. The conditions imposed upon him by the Patriarch of Jerusalem came vividly before his mind, and he told her of the difficulty ; but she so asserted her absolute chastity, that he could not but believe her, and wished to begin their flight at once.

But the old chamberlain, Boniface, had overheard them, and, disapproving of their plan, he gave them the benefit of his sage counsel. He pointed out that, if they fled now, the king would at once pursue them on his return from hunting, but that if, when the king came back, he were to go boldly into the hall, the king would inquire of him, as a stranger, what news he had.

> Ye shall tell him redely
> That ye came out of Surry,[1]
> And that the land is greatly noyed,[2]
> Townes be brent and men destroied,
> And that King Bradwyne is
> In point to lese[3] his landes ywis[4]
> Through Syrake and his men.

Now this counsel was feasible, as Bradwine was brother to Joure, and, having tied up Arundel, he went into hall, and things fell out as Boniface had suggested. The king had some doubts as to the truth of Bevis's story, thinking

[1] Syria.   [2] Disturbed.   [3] Lose.   [4] I thinke.

it strange that his brother should not have sent to him
to tell him of the straits he was in ; but, on Bevis asseve-
rating that it was perfectly true, he ordered his troops to
get ready, and set out to his brother's assistance. He left
Sir Grassy, his steward, in charge of home, but the wily
Boniface disposed of him, by giving him a sleeping draught.

They then took their flight; but when Sir Grassy awoke
next day, and found the queen had fled with the pseudo
palmer, he followed them with all the men of Mambraunt,
and surrounded the fugitives.   Sir Bevis felt that he,
Arundel, and Morglay, ought to be amusing themselves
in slaughtering this mob, but the wise Boniface would not
hear of it, and led them to a cave where they might be
hidden and secure; and so it happened.   Grassy searched
all about, and, finding no trace of them, went back with
his force home again.

But during their sojourn in the cave, food was scant—so
much so that Bevis had to leave Boniface and Josian, and
go and search for food.   During his absence two lions
visited the cave, and although Boniface made all the
resistance possible, they slew and devoured him and his
horse. Then, succumbing to the potent virtue of Josian
in her combined character of king's daughter and pure
maiden, they laid their heads in her lap, for they were
unable to harm her. A terrible sight greeted Bevis on his
return, but his joy was great when he saw Josian unhurt.
She calmly said :

> Come and venge me of these two,
> For right now have they slayne
> Bonyface your chamberlayne ;
> The one lyon will I holde
> Whyles ye make the other cold.

This mastery over the lions, and the utter absence of fear of them, convinced Bevis of Josian's purity ; but it was not in his nature to have his adventures made easy for him, so he desired that both should be loosed on him at once.

> Strong and perylous was that fyght
> Betwene the lyons and the knyght ;
> They gave him woundes longe and wyde,
> His armure they tare on every syde.

But at last he slew them both with one stroke of his sword. A little time was devoted to grief for Boniface, and they continued on their journey, which was not destined to be uneventful ; for they had not gone far before they met with a giant, who, as he plays a somewhat important part in this history, had better be described in the chronicler's own words :

> He was bothe myghty and stronge,
> He was full thyrty fote longe,
> He was brystled like a sowe,
> A fote there was betwene each brow ;
> His lipes were great, they hanged syde,[1]
> His eies were holow, his mouth wide ;
> He was lothely to loke on,
> He was lyker a dyvell than a man ;
> His staffe was a yonge oke,
> He would geve a great stroke.

[1] Aside.

Sir Bevis asked this portentous being what he called himself; he replied that his name was Ascaparte, and that he had been sent by Sir Grassy to bring back the runaways, that he was delighted to have met with them, and would, after binding them, lead them to Mambraunt. But this was not Bevis's way; so, lighting from Arundel, whom he gave to Josian to hold, he assailed Ascaparte with Morglay, and, being light and active, skipped hither and thither, dealing the giant wounds, which, from his unwieldiness, he was unable to parry, whilst his own strokes fell harmless. At last, making a mighty blow, he slipped and fell, and Sir Bevis at once was ready to cut off his head; but Josian, who evidently had a fashionable lady's eye for a tall footman, begged her lover not to kill him.

> Syr, she sayd, ye shall him save,
> And let him live and be your knave.[1]
> Dame, he sayd, he wyll us betraye,
> I will be borowe[2] he sayde naye.
> Ascaparte made Bevis homage,
> And became Syr Bevis' page.

They journeyed on until they came to the sea, where they found a merchant ship ready to sail for Christendom, but the Saracens therein did not care to receive Sir Bevis and Josian, and Ascaparte had to clear them all out, which he did with very little trouble. Then, tucking Arundel and Sir Bevis under one arm, and Josian under

---

[1] Man-servant.   [2] I will pledge myself.

the other, he stalked on board, hoisted the sail, and, in course of time, arrived at Cologne.

SIR BEVIS FIGHTS AND OVERCOMES ASCAPARTE.

Here he found a relative, in the person of the bishop, who turned out to be a brother of Sir Sabere, and, consequently, his uncle ; and of course, under such favourable conditions, his first care was to get Josian baptized, and in answer to the bishop's inquiry as to who this lady was—

> Syr, sayd Bevis, of hethenesse a quene ;
> For her I have suffred muche payne,
> And she wolde become christen fayne.

ASCAPARTE CARRIES SIR BEVIS AND JOSIAN ON BOARD SHIP.

> He sayde, what is he this bad visage ?
> Syr, sayd Bevis, he is my page,
> I pray you chrysten him also,
> Though he be both blacke and blo.

The byshope christened Josian
That was as white as any swan,
For Ascaparte was made a tonne ;[1]
And whan he shoulde therein be donne,
He lepet over upon the benche,
And said, churle, wilt thou me drenche,
The devyll of hell thy bayne[2] be ;
I am to muche to be christned, I tel y^e.
The folke had good game and loughe,
But the byshope was wroth ynoughe.

During his stay in Cologne, he prevented himself from
rusting, and did good to the inhabitants of that district
by slaying a dragon.   He started on this adventure with
Ascaparte, but the great lubber had no pluck, and returned
home after having heard the dragon yell.   The description
of the fight takes up many pages.   At last he

. . . hit him under the winge
As he was in his flienge.
There he was tender, without scale,
And Bevis thought to be his bale.
He smote after as I you say
With his good sworde Morglay.
Up to the hylter Morglay yode,[3]
Through herte, lyver, bone and bloude.

Then, cutting off the dragon's head, he stuck it on a
spear, and bore it to the town, where the inhabitants
received him with enthusiasm, and gave him an ovation.

Having thus propitiated the people and bishop of
Cologne, he asked the latter's assistance to avenge his
father's death, and he was promised a hundred men-at-

[1] Barrel, or cask for his immersion.   [2] Bane.   [3] Went.

arms at the bishop's cost and maintenance. As the enterprise was somewhat hazardous, he left Josian behind him, and set forth with his company. On his arrival near Hampton he sent a messenger to Sir Murdure to say that a knight of Brittany, named Sir Gararde, with a goodly company, had come thither, understanding that he was going to war with another knight, and that, if he would, they would help him, or, if not, they would join the other side.

Needless to say Sir Murdure was glad of such aid, and welcomed Sir Bevis heartily. His mother, not knowing who he was, feasted him, and Sir Murdure regaled his guest with a very garbled version of Sir Sabere's en-deavours to reassert his nephew's rights: after hearing which, our hero was in strange doubt whether to slay Sir Murdure there, or go away from him. If he did the one, he would be counted guilty of treachery ; if the other, of cowardice; so he decided to slay him in open fight ; but to do this he had recourse to stratagem. He told Sir Murdure that his men had left their horses and armour behind them, and begged him to furnish them with these necessaries as well as shipping to take them to the Isle of Wight, where Sir Sabere was. Sir Murdure found them, and Sir Bevis sailed, thus furnished at the enemy's expense, to join his uncle. Sir Sabere recognized his nephew's cognizance, and met him with effusion. A messenger was found, bold enough to go to the felon Murdure, and tell him that Sir Gararde was, in truth, Sir Bevis, who meant to avenge his father's death, and win back his own heritage. Sir Murdure was in such an ungovernable rage at these tidings that he threw his knife at the messenger, but, missing him, the blade was buried in the breast of his own son, killing him on the spot; whilst the messenger, taking advantage of the uproar, jumped on his horse and escaped.

The story now turns on the fortunes of Josian, who was left at Cologne. An earl named Myle cast loving eyes upon her, and left her not long without disclosing his passion for her; and, when he would fain have possessed her, by fair means or foul, she told him that, if he tried the latter, she would hand him over to Ascaparte. The earl knew how to deal with a thick-witted giant, and sent the latter a letter purporting to come from Bevis, in which he bade his page meet him at a certain castle. The unreasoning mountain of flesh at once set out, arrived at the castle, went inside, and was duly locked in.

The earl lost no time in conveying this news to Josian, and she sent a statement of her position by a messenger to Sir Bevis, and then, when the earl next came a-wooing, she promised to be his bride, and, what is more, next day they were married. But, on the wedding night, when they were retiring to rest, and had received the then usual visits of their friends and guests—

> Syr, sayd Josian, fayre love myne,
> Let no person herein be
> This night to here our privite,

> Neyther knyght, mayden, nor swayne,
> Myselfe shal be your chamberlayne.
> He sayd, lemman, it shal be so ;
> Both man and maiden he made out go,
> He shet the dore well and fast,
> And set hym downe at the last.
> There was a curtayne as it was lawe[1]
> Before the bed it was drawe,
> Than, on her gyrdel, withouten lesinge
> She made a knot rydyng ;
> About his necke she drewe it thore
> And strangled hym withouten more,
> Then on a beme she hanged him hye.

Josian slept soundly and late, and the barons, &c., came to the door to rouse the sluggards, when Josian pointed to the swinging corpse, and confessed it to be her deed. Swiftly did her punishment fall upon her. She was condemned to be burnt at a stake, on the morrow, outside the town. The glare of the fire caught Ascaparte's eyes, and, a glimmer of sense coming through his dull brain, he burst out of the castle, and, seizing a fisherman's boat, he came to land, where the first to greet him was Sir Bevis, who asked him where was Josian ? and he stammered out an excuse that Earl Myle had betrayed him.

There was no time for parley, but onwards they sped ; and, indeed, they came not a moment too soon, for the fire was ready, and Josian was there.

> In her smocke she stode therby,
> Right as they shoulde her brenne.

[1] Hung.

Bevis, with Morglay, and Arundel, and Ascaparte, soon made mincemeat of Earl Myle's friends, and they all took their departure for the Isle of Wight, where Sir Sabere heartily welcomed them.

Sir Bevis sought and obtained recruits, but so did the other side. An army came from Almaine, seven thousand men from Scotland, and Sir Murdure had three thousand of his own. Judging these to be sufficient, they took ship to the Isle of Wight. Sir Sabere's troops were divided into three commands, whereof he took three thousand, Sir Bevis three, and Ascaparte was trusted with another three thousand. The fight was obstinate, and Bevis endeavoured to single out Sir Murdure. Once he succeeded in wounding him, but he was rescued. Ascaparte now came up, with his contingent all fresh, and the enemy were greatly afraid of his huge stature. Sir Bevis recommended him to pay particular attention to a knight on a white horse, who was Sir Murdure, and to capture him by all means, and bring him to the castle.

Away went the giant, and the road he took was made plain by the dead and dying, whom his mighty staff laid low. There was the knight on the white horse before him; in another moment horse and knight were tucked up under the arm of the giant, whose huge form was now the centre of the battle. The King of Scotland came to the rescue of Sir Murdure, Sir Bevis hurried to the help of Ascaparte, and fiercely the battle waged. Yet Ascaparte's mighty strength prevailed, and Sir Murdure was safely lodged in the castle. The capture of their leader dispirited Murdure's hosts ; they hesitated, broke, and fled, chased by Sir Bevis and Sir Sabere with fearful slaughter, the King of Scotland only, with a trusty few, escaping in a ship.

They had now a little leisure to bestow on Sir Murdure, and his fate was evidently intended as a warning to those who might be like minded.

> Syr Bevis without any let
> Made a caudron on the fyre be set
> Full of pyche and of brymstone :
> A worse death was never none.
> Whan the caudron boyled harde
> Murdure was caste in the mydwarde,
> That deth died he seckerly [1]
> For the deth of good Syr Guy.
> Thereof hearde the countesse
> That Syr Murdure dede was,
> She stode above in a towre,
> So wo she was for Syr Murdure
> That she fell downe and broke her necke.
> I beshrew him that therof doth recke.[2]

Now, there was nothing left for the heir but to enter into the heritage he had so hardly won, and he set out for Hampton, where he was met by the burgesses, who brought him to his castle. Here all the subsidiary barons did him homage, and the one thing necessary to his happiness was also attainable.

> Than Bevis, he, sothe to sayne,
> Sent after the byshop of Coleyne

[1] Surely.   [2] I pity him who cares about it.

That he woulde for anithinge
To be at his weddinge.
Whan the bysshope was ther come,
Two knights had Josian anone ;
To Churche than they her ledde,
The Bysshope him selfe on the boke red,
And to Bevis was wedded blyve [1]
To the endynge of theyr lyve.

Here, according to modern ethics, the history should end. Sir Bevis had apparently gained his heart's desire, but the old chronicler has much more to tell about him.

First, acting under the advice of his uncle Sabere, he went to London to do homage to King Edgar, who not only confirmed him in his earldom of Hampton, but made him Earl Marshal, a dignity formerly borne by his father. This visit, however, was to have an unhappy influence over the future life of Sir Bevis. And it happened in this way. Whilst at King Edgar's Court,

In Somer at Whitsontyde,
Whan Knights most on horsbacke ride,
A cours let they make on a daye
Stedes and palfrayes for to assaye
Whiche horse that best may ren.
Thre myles the cours was then ;
Who that might ryd shoulde
Have. rī. ī'. of red golde.

Sir Bevis, confident in the super-excellence of Arundel, entered him for this race, and, coming on the day appointed, found his competitors had already started, and had got some half-mile ahead. But Arundel, even thus heavily

[1] Quickly.

handicapped, soon caught up, and passed his rivals, winning the race by a long distance.

The king's son coveted this incomparable steed, and wished to buy him of Bevis, but he refused to part with him on any consideration. So the prince determined to take him, and, going to Arundel's stable, attempted to lead him forth; but one kick from that animal scattered his brains—a fate which King Edgar so took to heart that he called his parliament together, and demanded that Bevis should be slain, by being torn asunder by wild beasts. But the barons withstood him, saying that Bevis had nought to do with his son's death, but that, if any victim was necessary, Arundel should clearly be it.

But Bevis loved his horse so, that he proposed a course which was agreed to, which was, that if Arundel were spared, he would give up his heritage and honours to Sir Sabere, and banish himself from England. A fortnight's grace was allowed him, but if at the expiration of that time he were still in England, " he shoulde be taken and faste bounde."

Sadly he rode to Hampton, and at once set about the preparations for his departure. Humbly he went forth with Josian, having only Ascaparte for retinue, whilst Terry, his cousin, accompanied them presumably for companionship. Better had it been if Ascaparte had been left behind, for the fallen fortunes of his master had materially altered the giant's feelings towards him.

Ascaparte that false thefe
For hym Bevis was in muche grefe ;
He thought I dwel here without fail,
I get nought elles but great travayl,
And I myght be Termagaunte.
Bring Josyon to Mambraunte,
Full welcome should I be yᵉ king tyll,[1]
And have ynoughe at my wyll.
This Ascaparte false was he,
For Bevis was fallen in poverte.
Whan a man in poverte is fall,
Few frendes meteth he withall.

What made this exile the worse was, that Josian was
very near her confinement, which happened when they
were in a forest. Bevis and Terry had built a hut for her,
and when her time came, she begged them so earnestly to
go away from her for a while, that they could not but obey
her. She was delivered of twins (boys), and then the
wretch Ascaparte, who had given Bevis and Terry the slip,
and had returned—

To the lodge wente he there,
And Josian awaye did bere.
There might no praiers her borowe,[2]
I wonder her hart burst not for sorow,
For he swore by Termagaunte
He woulde her lede to Mambraunte.

Bevis, on his return, was thunderstruck to find Josian
gone, and the twin babes in her place, but he soon came to
the conclusion that it was Ascaparte's doings, and fainted
away. On his recovery, he took off his mantle, and, wrap-

[1] Thereof.   [2] Avail.

ping his babes therein, set off, with Terry, in pursuit of
Ascaparte.   On their way they met a forester, who could
give them no news ; but he agreed to take one of the children, and bring it up for seven years, when he was to take
it to Sir Bevis.   They next met a fisherman, with exactly
similar results, and, being thus " without encumbrance,"
Bevis and Terry went on their way.

They came to a castellated town, in which they stayed
at an inn, where Bevis, looking out of a window, saw preparations for a tournament.   On inquiry he found that the
lord of that town, who was dying, and his daughter
unmarried, this tournament was instituted, so that the
strongest and best knight was to have her hand and her
lands for the prize.   The temptation of a fight was so
great, that Bevis asked Terry if they should joust for that
lady, and Terry, being of a kindred spirit, consented.
Needless to say, they overthrew all comers, and Sir Bevis
was adjudged the best knight.   Dame Elynor (for that was
the lady's name) immediately proposed their marriage, but
when she learned from Bevis his melancholy story, they
agreed that they should live in Platonic friendship for
seven years, and if at the end of that time no tidings could
be heard of Josian, they were to be married.   Meantime
Bevis was governor of the land.

But how fared it with Josian whilst her lord was thus
unmindful of her ?   Luckily for her, Sir Sabere had a gift
of dreaming, and he dreamt that Bevis had been slain

by Ascaparte; and, so vivid was the vision, that he felt convinced that harm had befallen his beloved nephew. So, with twelve knights, disguised as palmers, but mail clad, and well armed under their pilgrim's weeds, they set out, and, going into Heathenesse, they came upon Ascaparte and Josian near the city of Mambraunt. Josian appealed to the palmer, Sir Sabere, for succour, and not without avail, for they all fell on Ascaparte and killed him.

The giant being dead, their next thoughts were to find Sir Bevis; and that Josian might not be annoyed in her journeying by men admiring her beauty, Sir Sabere provided for

> Her body that was so fayre and gent : [1]
> He noynted it with an oyntment,
> And made her to seme yelowe and grene
> That was before so fayre and shene,
> That no man should take her him fro
> Therfore discoloured her so.

They wandered about for some time without hearing any tidings of Bevis, until they came to a city where Sir Sabere accidentally met with his son Terry. Mutual explanations ensued. Josian's ointment was removed; she was re-united to Bevis; her children were sent for, and came. Sir Terry married Dame Elynor, and once more, according to our ideas, the story ought to come to an end. But no! It is carried back, and shows that King Joure, having been unable to find any traces of Bevis and Josian, vented his

[1] Gentle, or soft.

wrath upon King Ermine, and gave him battle. A pilgrim told Bevis the news, and he, his two sons, Guy and Myles, and Sir Sabere, accompanied by a goodly company of knights, went forth to Armony.

This array somewhat frightened the old king, especially as he remembered the treacherous trick he had served Sir Bevis, so he cried him mercy a hundred times, and promised, if he would but forgive him, he would turn Christian. This was accepted, and the Bishop of Rome was applied to to send clergy; which he gladly did, who baptized not only the king, but all his people. This being satisfactorily done, Sir Joure began to be aggressive, and, having got together an army of forty thousand Saracens, he invaded Armony, and wasted it with fire and sword. At length the opposing forces met, and a terrible fight ensued. Bevis, with Morglay in hand, was as usual irresistible, and he left heaps of dead Saracens upon the field. At last, King Joure being taken prisoner and his host overpowered, they fled, being slaughtered in their flight. King Joure had, in prison, time for reflection, the upshot of which was a desire to be released, and to that end

> King Joure prayed Bevis tho
> That he might make raunsome and go,
> And for his raunsome yf he wolde
> Twenty sommers of red golde,
> And thre hundreth beddes of sylke,
> An hundreth stedes as whyt as mylke,

An hundreth cuppes of golde fyne
And as many of Misculyne : [1]
All this raunsome I wyll thee gyve
Yf thou nowe let me lyve.
Bevis said make thi servant it bring,
And I shall save thy life, syr king ;
So muche dred I not the,
But I lefer have y^r treasure than thee.

King Ermine, finding his end drawing nigh, sent for Guy, Sir Bevis's eldest son, and made over the kingdom of Armony to him. Then the old man died, and Sir Sabere, longing to see his wife and children, went to England.

Bevis had suffered from misplaced lenity in Ascaparte ; he had now to have a repetition of the lesson in King Joure, who coveted the horse Arundel, and would fain steal it. He had a fitting tool in a horse thief named Robson, who went to Armony, and, with his charms and craft, beguiled poor Arundel, whose loss left his master inconsolable. Here Sir Sabere's accomplishment of dreaming, again was of great use. He had a vision of Sir Bevis riding Arundel, that the horse threw him, and broke two of his ribs. So satisfied was he that this dream portended evil, that he set out, wella rmed, to Mambraunt, and there, by a river, he saw Robson on Arundel. He spoke fairly to the thief, but, seizing his opportunity, he jumped up behind him, and slew him.

After killing the infidel, Sir Sabere turned Arundel's

[1] Mixed metal.

head towards Armony, followed by some three thousand Saracens. Josian was in a tower, and, seeing some one riding Arundel and thus pursued, told Bevis, who, with his two sons and his cousin Terry, and all his knights, sallied forth, rescued Sir Sabere, and annihilated the Saracens.

King Joure, naturally, was displeased at the course events were taking, and sent to ask counsel of his brother Bradwine, King of Syria, who advised him to challenge Bevis to single combat, and thus end the strife—the victor to have the other's lands. With Morglay's assistance King Joure was killed, and Bevis, putting on his armour, went on, at once, to Mambraunt; and the people of that city, thinking it was their king returned, opened their gates, and, in consequence, were easily subdued. They were soon reconciled to their new ruler, and not only did homage to him, but they "cursed their mawmetry," [1] and were baptized into Christianity, those who would not conform to the new regulations being immediately slain.

One day, whilst Bevis and Sir Sabere were hawking, a messenger came to them, and reported that King Edgar had, by counsel of his steward, disinherited Sir Sabere's son, who was Bevis's heir. This could not be borne, and the whole family, with ten thousand men, set forth for England, and landed at Hampton ; and there they found the news to be true, that Edgar, at the instigation of Sir Bryan of Cornwall, an inveterate enemy of Sir Bevis, had

---

[1] Mammet—an idol, puppet, or doll.

seized upon Bevis's estate, in satisfaction of Arundel having killed his son.

Bevis and his host marched on London, and encamped at Putney, where leaving them, he, with twelve knights only, went to King Edgar, and asked him why he had disinherited Sir Sabere and his son. The king, at first, treated him kindly, telling him, if wrong had been done him, it should be remedied by Parliament; but, over-persuaded by Sir Bryan, he came to no definite conclusion. Sir Bevis left the presence without redress, and Sir Bryan made a cry throughout the city, assembling all who could bear arms. The city gates were locked, and chains drawn across the street.

Bevis bade his men to make their way to Putney, and to tell his sons to come to his aid, and then, leaping on Arundel, he "went for" Sir Bryan, and clove him from the crown to the saddle, and killed some two hundred of the citizens. He then turned into Bread Street, where he met many Lombards, who assaulted him, and got slain for their pains. In Chepe, too, was a bloody fight, some six hundred men here perishing, and there was fighting all that summer's night.

The knights reached Putney safely, and told their news. Josian swooned, but the men folk hastened to the succour of their chief—Guy arming himself with a sword that once belonged to Lancelot du Lac, and Myles having the famous brand Duvandel, once the property of Roland. They crossed the Thames, effected an entrance into the city at Ludgate, and they found Sir Bevis, weary indeed, but still fighting. Guy came in time to kill a "doughty Lombard," who was pressing his father, and this he did with such good will that it quite revived Sir Bevis, and even Arundel neighed loudly, "and helped Bevis for to fight." It was a terrible fight—

> So harde they gan together mete
> That the blode raune in every strete ;
> So many men was dead
> The Chepe syde was of blode red,
> For there was slayne, I understand,
> To the number of thirty thousande.

The fighting having ceased, they retired to Putney, and thence to Hampton, where they awaited the king's forces, which they fully expected would be sent to punish them ; but the king told his barons all that this strife was entirely caused by Sir Bryan, who was dead : that Bevis was a man of war, the king himself was getting old, and he thought the best thing to do was to give his daughter in marriage to Sir Bevis's son Myles, whom he would make Earl of Cornwall ; and this was duly done, amidst great rejoicings.

After these festivities Bevis and Josian retired to Mambraunt, and dwelt there seven years, until they died. Their end was peaceful, a contrast to their lives.

> Than waxed Josian seke and laye,[1]
> And Bevis also as I you saye ;

[1] Took to her bed.

Bishopes and friers came to them blyve [1]
Bevis and Josian for to shryve.
Whan Bevis and Josian the good
Had themselfe humbled to god in moode,
Eyther turned to other without bost
And both they yielded up the ghost.

   ✻   ✻   ✻   ✻   ✻

Syr Guy than to the stable went he
Arundel his horse for to se,
Whan he came there no sound he read
For Arundell there found he deade ;
Syr Guy thought marveyle y^e south to saye
For all they dyed upon a daye.

   ✻   ✻   ✻   ✻   ✻

Thus endeth Bevis of South Hampton,
King and Knight of great renowne.

[1] Quietly.

Syr Tryamoure.

Sír Tryamoure.

EARLY MSS. of this Romance are scarce. There is one in the Public Library of the University of Cambridge, which has been edited by Halliwell for the Percy Society, and another is given in the Percy MSS. Of printed copies but two are known to exist, both printed by Copland, one in the Bodleian Library, and the other in the British Museum, and from the latter I have taken my story.

The name of the kingdom over which Aradas was sovereign, was Arragon, but when he reigned we shall probably never know; nor is it material in order to follow out this history. He was blessed with a queen whom he loved dearly, by name Margarete, and they seem to have lived a blissful existence, marred only by one drawback—

> Thys kynge loved well his quene,
> Bycause she was semely to sene,
> And as true as the turtel on tree ;
> Ether to other made grete mone,
> For chyldren together had they none ;

and this so preyed upon the king, that he made a vow to
go and fight the heathen in the Holy Land, hoping, by so
doing, to find favour with the Deity, who might, perhaps,
grant him the dearest wish of his heart.   The queen did
her best to combat this resolution, but neither her tears
nor entreaties could prevail, and the king set out on his
crusade, leaving his wife to the special charge of his steward
Marrocke.   Now this Marrocke was a false and specious
traitor, and no sooner was the king's back turned, than he
fell to a wooing of the queen on his own account ; but she
scornfully rejected all his advances, and when he pestered
her still more, she threatened to have him hanged on the
gallows.   Then he no longer persecuted her, but he vowed
to be avenged.

The king performed prodigies of valour in the Holy
Land, and made a very short campaign, returning after
only a few months' absence ; and his joy at his coming
home was marvellously enhanced by finding his wife
enceinte.

> Many tymes he dyd her kysse,
> And made grete joye wythoute mysse,
> His hert made great rejoicyng.

But this was of short duration, for the villain Marrocke
assured the king that his queen had been unfaithful to him,
and that he, in the interests of his master, had slain her
paramour.   At this news the king sorrowed greatly, but
seems to have had no doubt whatever as to the truth of

his steward's story, and to have judged her without the smallest inquiry, debating whether he should not at once burn her. Marrocke, however, was against this, and suggested banishment.

> Delyver her an ambelynge stede,
> And an olde knyght her to lede.

This advice was followed, and thus the wicked steward carried out the sentence on the queen, who meekly, but sorrowfully—a very patient Griselda—suffered her unjust doom.

> He dyd her clothe in purple wede,
> And sette her on an olde stede,
> That was both croked and almost blynd.
> He toke her an olde knyght,
> Kynne to the quene, and Syr Roger hyght
> That was bothe curteyse and kynd ;
> Thre dayes he gave them leve to passe,
> And after that daye set was,
> If men myght them fynde
> The quene sholde be brent stercke [1] dede
> In a fyre with flames rede.
> This came of the stuardes mynde,
> Forty florens for theyr expence
> The kyng had given them in this presence.

And so they set out on their sorrowful journey, the queen weeping, and the old knight comforting her as best he might. No servants accompanied them ; there were but they twain and a noble greyhound belonging to Sir Roger. Slowly, too, they went, and on this the wicked Marrocke

---

[1] Stark, stiff.

counted, for he got together a band of his own men, and
having got in front of the exiles, he lay in wait for them,
his object being to kill the knight and possess himself of
the queen. When, therefore, they came near, he and his
men showed themselves, declaring their intentions. The
old knight laid about him manfully, and accounted for fourteen of the caitiff band, and in this he was well seconded
by his greyhound, who "full bytterly gan byte." But
Marrocke got behind the old knight, and, piercing his back
with a spear, killed him.

Meanwhile, the queen, having a wholesome dread of the
steward, fled, and hid herself in a green grove, so that when
Marrocke, after killing Sir Roger, sought her, she was
nowhere to be found, and, after hacking the knight's body,
he was fain to return home. The queen, having mourned
awhile over the corpse of Sir Roger, which the faithful
greyhound would not quit, went on her way towards
Hungary, until her condition forbade her to go any farther,
and, having alighted in a forest and tied her horse to a
tree, a boy was born to her, which filled her with a deep
joy, and, having attended to it and wrapped it up well, they
both fell asleep.

A good knight named Sir Barnarde Mausewynge was
hunting the deer, and came riding past where these two lay.
Alighting from his horse, he approached the sleeping lady,
and awoke her, asking her how she came in that condition.
She told him some portion of her story, and then the kind

knight lifted her up courteously, and, carrying the child, led her to his castle, where he handed her over to female care, and she was put to bed.

The child was afterwards christened Tryamoure, and at his baptism received many rich gifts from the neighbouring lords and ladies. And there for some years Margarete and her child abode.

> Of her they were never wery.
> The chylde was taught grete nurture,
> A mayster hym had under his cure
> And taught him curtesye.
> This chylde waxed wonderous well,
> Of grete stature bothe fleshe and fell,
> Every man loved hym truely;
> Of his company all folke were gladde,
> None other cause in dede they hadde,
> The chylde was gentyll and bolde.

We left the greyhound by the side of his dead master, whose wounds he lay and licked, until the body became somewhat decomposed, when he scratched a grave, and dragging the corpse into it, covered it with earth and moss. Neither heat nor cold, nor the winter storm, nor man's hand, could make the faithful hound relinquish his guard over his master's grave, which he quitted but once a day in order to provide himself with food. And this went on for seven long years, when the dog waxed old, and game became so scarce that one day he sought food in the king's hall, where all the barons and knights were set at meat; and having obtained it, he looked all round as if he sought some one, and, being unable to find him, he went away once more to his master's grave.

This conduct he repeated on another day, and it so excited the king's curiosity, that he asked whether that was not Sir Roger's dog, who went forth with the queen and that knight ; remarking that if it were so, they should soon have tidings of the pair, and ordered that he should be followed when next he made his appearance. On his next visit to the royal hall the hound saw whom he wanted. The false villain Marrocke was there, and, springing at his throat, the dog bit it asunder, and thus ended the foul life of the caitiff steward.

> But than he wolde not byde,
> For to his grave he ranne,
> There followed hym many a manne,
> Some on hors and some besyde ;
> And whan he came wher his mayster was
> He layde hym downe upon the grasse
> And barked at the menne agayne.
> There myght no man hym from ye place gete,
> And yet with staves they dyd hym bete
> That he was almost slayne.

The men returned and reported the dog's behaviour to the king, whose acumen perceived its cause—that Marrocke had slain Sir Roger, and slandered the queen, and sent them again, with instructions to dig. This they did, and found the old knight's body in a wonderful state of preservation. They bore it to the king, who shed bitter and unavailing tears over it, and, as some reparation towards

the dead, and to his libelled and exiled queen, he had
Marrocke's body drawn through the city and then hanged
on a tree, that all men might see one that had wrought
such treason. Sir Roger's body was re-interred in a more
fitting place, in a sumptuous manner, but the greyhound
still was faithful to his old master, and kept guard over his
new tomb until he died.

The next thing the king did was to try and find his
injured queen ; but, though he sent far and near, he could
hear no tidings of her, and for many years he lived a life
of sorrow and remorse, mourning and weeping, for that he
had sent her forth innocent and misjudged, and, worse than
all else, was ignorant of her fate.

When Tryamoure was fourteen years old, he excelled all
of his age in size and strength, in good looks, and martial
exercises, and it so happened that at this time died, at a
great age, the King of Hungary, leaving as his successor
his daughter " Fayre Elyne," who was fourteen years of
age. The country around was unquiet, and her counsellors
advised that she should marry some mighty prince, who,
by his personal prowess, might be able to defend her
kingdom against all comers ; and for that purpose a great
jousting was commanded, to take place in six months' time,
which would sift the competitors for this great prize. The
fame of this great tournament reached to the ends of the
civilized world, and lords and knights from all parts
flocked to Hungary.

Even Tryamoure heard of it, and his youthful heart beat high, as to what he might accomplish, could he but be at the jousting ; but how could he go thither without horse or armour ?—and he pondered night and morn how to gratify his wish. At length he bethought him of Syr Barnerde, and he boldly asked that knight to lend him horse and armour, so that he might go to the tourney. Sir Barnerde told him that he knew nothing of jousting, and was not able to wield the necessary weapons ; but the precocious lad replying, that there was no knowing what he could do till he tried, the knight's scruples gave way, and he promised the loan of arms and steed : moreover, that he would accompany him. This rejoiced the lad's heart exceedingly, but, when he asked his mother's blessing, there was somewhat of a scene with that fond parent, who for the first time was to be parted from her darling ; but at length she acquiesced, and must have felt proud of her boy, who, when armed, and on horseback, looked every inch a man.

So Sir Barnerde and Tryamoure rode to the jousting, and there took the side of the King of Arragon, who had been attracted to the jousts, not knowing that he was the boy's father. Needless to say that Tryamoure overthrew every knight opposed to him, and Sir Barnerde failed not, on every such event, to shout "A Tryamoure! A Tryamoure!" calling special attention to our hero's prowess. He even had a course with his father, and unhorsed him. In

short, he was the hero of the tournament, having kept
the lists against all comers for three days, and was therefore entitled to the hand and lands of the fair Elyne, who
looked upon him with decided eyes of favour.

But, among the knights he had overthrown was Sir
James, son of the Emperor of Germany ; and, as he left
the lists, Sir James laid wait for him privily, and riding
at Tryamoure, with a spear, pierced his thigh, and almost
killed him ; but Tryamoure had strength enough left to
strike him one blow, which made Sir James a corpse.
The German prince's followers immediately set upon
Tryamoure, and it would have gone hard with him, had not
King Aradas, by a lucky chance, come up and rescued him.

Sir Barnerde saw him home, but, when Queen Margarete
beheld her wounded darling, she fainted, and, on her
recovery, sensibly sent for a doctor.

Meanwhile the morrow came, but with it no victor to
claim his prize, as should have been ; and the lords and
knights who were assembled, begged the princess to choose
from among them, as Tryamoure had not thought it worth
while to exercise his right. They sought right and left
for him, and all supposed he had ridden home. But the
princess had seen quite enough of him to love him, and, in
spite of all the pressure put upon her by the lords and
knights, she would have none of them, nor would she
make a choice among them until a year had passed. To
this they were fain to accede, and so they rode their

different ways, leaving the fair Elyne more bent than
ever on having Tryamoure for her husband.

Sir James's men bore the corpse of their master to his
father's court, and, in reply to the emperor's question,
they could only tell him that the name of him who had
slain his son was Tryamoure, but where he dwelt they
knew not ; but of this they were certain, that the King of
Arragon came and helped him against themselves ; and
the emperor, sore at his son's death, vowed vengeance on
both of them. He gathered together a great array, and
marched on Arragon, and, the king having fled to a strong
castle, he lay siege to it. In those days, however, sieges
took time, especially if the defenders behaved like Aradas,
who treated the besiegers

> With gounes [1] and grete stones rounde
> Were throwen downe to the grounde,
> And on the men were caste,
> They brake many backes and bones ;
> Thus they fought every daye ones
> Whyle seven wekes did laste.

Neither side cared about this, and King Aradas sent
two lords to the Emperor of Germany, to try and nego-
tiate a peace. They told the emperor, what was perfectly
true, that Aradas had nothing to do with the death of his
son—in fact that he was killed before the king came up ;
but, if the emperor still felt aggrieved, the king would
meet him in single combat, and so settle the matter ; or,

---

[1] Engines—such as catapults, &c.

if that were not agreeable, it might be arranged vicariously, by means of two champions. This proposition was agreed to, a date fixed upon for the combat, and a truce entered into. The German champion was a giant named Maradas, and Aradas put his trust in procuring the assistance of the doughty Tryamoure; but, although he sent messengers all ways in search of him, no tidings of him could be gathered.

Meanwhile, Tryamoure's wound had healed, and he was once more stout and strong, when one day he astonished his mother by asking who his father was ; but the only answer she gave him was, that he should know when he married the Princess Elyne. This not satisfying him, he bade his mother farewell, as he was going to set out in search of adventures. He took the way to Arragon, and was accompanied by three greyhounds, with which he hunted as he rode. He was thus once following a hart, when he was confronted by fourteen foresters, who swore they would hale him to prison, such being the law of that land. But when they began to apply physical force to enforce their argument, Tryamoure got wroth, and soon killed some, wounded others, and the rest fled. He then went on in his pursuit of the hart, which had slain two of his greyhounds, was sore pressing the third, and would probably have killed it also, had not Tryamoure come up, and slain the deer with a spear-thrust ; and, as was customary in venerie, he put his horn to his lips, and blew a " mort."

King Aradas and his knights were in hall when they

heard the sound of that horn, and were sorely wondering thereat, when in rushed a forester, who explained that there was a gentleman hunting the deer, who had beaten their whole force, killing some and wounding others. The king, whose thoughts were of a personal nature, for the time of finding a substitute had nigh run out, replied that he had great need of such a man, and bade them go and bring him in, using all courtesy. This was done, Tryamoure, on the way, learning that he whom he was about to visit was Aradas, the King of Arragon. As soon as he saw the king, he recognized him; but the king took him by the hand and welcomed him, begging to know his name. He replied Tryamoure, and called to the king's recollection how he had come to his assistance when he was in sore need. So overjoyed was Aradas at this unexpected rencontre, that he fainted three times.

When he had recovered himself, he poured into Tryamoure's listening ear the story of his woes—how that the very help he had afforded him was wrought to his undoing, for with the death of the emperor's son he had nothing to do.

> Then sayd Tryamoure, tho
> That ye for me have been greved so,
> If I myght it amende,
> And at the daye of batyll
> I trust to prove my myght well,
> If God will grace me sende.
> Than was Kynge Aradas very gladde,
> And of Maradas he was not adradde.[1]

[1] Afraid.

Tryamoure was the king's guest until the day of battle, when he was made a knight, and they went together to the place of combat. It was a fearful fight, for they were evenly matched, but a blow of Tryamoure's sword falling short, it killed the giant's horse. Maradas taunted him—

> . . . It is great shame
> On a stede to wreke his game,
> Thou sholdest rather to smyte me.

Tryamoure alighted from his horse to make the combat more even, and, remembering that he had only that day been made a knight, determined to prove himself worthy of the honour, and laid on with such good will, that he fairly tired out the giant, and, catching him off his guard, ran him through the body. The emperor, although "a sory man," made peace, according to his compact, kissed the king in token of amity, and, with his army, wended his way home. As, also, did King Aradas and Sir Tryamoure. Needless to say, the king dearly loved the knight, would always have him near him, and fain would make him his heir ; but this Sir Tryamoure declined, as he still remembered his princess in Hungary. With deep regret, the king allowed him to depart, furnishing him with costly arms, and a good steed, and so he took his leave.

As he went on his way, he met a palmer, in a mountain pass, who asked him for alms, which Sir Tryamoure gave him, accompanied "with wordes swete." The grateful pilgrim, in return, begged him to turn back, as there were two giants guarding that pass ; but that news seems to have gladdened our hero's heart, for

> In fayth, sayd Tryamoure, yf there be no mo,
> I truste in God that waye to go,

and continued on his journey, followed by the prayers of the palmer.

When he judged he had gone a sufficient distance, he blew his horn, and had not ridden far, when he saw two giants on a hill, one of whom rode towards him, whilst the other stopped where he was. The two met, and the usual combat took place, but it lasted so long that the second giant rose up, and, stopping the fight for a while, said to Sir Tryamoure,

> So doughty a knyght knowe I none,
> Thy name that thou us tell.
> Tryamoure sayd, fyrst will I wete [1]
> Why that you do kepe thys strete,
> And where that ye do dwell.
> They sayd, we had a brother hyght Maradas,
> With the Emperoure forsothe he was.
> A stronge man well I knowe
> In Aragon before the Emperoure,
> A knight men called hym Syr Tryamoure,
> In batayle there hym slewe.
> And also we say anoder,
> Burlongee, our elder broder,
> As a man of muche myght,
> He hath besyeged sothely
> The kynges doughter of Houngry,
> To wedde her he hath he hyght ;

[1] Know.

And so well hath he spedde
That he shall that lady wedde
But she may fynde a knyghte
That Burlonge overcome maye ;
For that same Tryamoure
Loved that lady par amoure,
As it is before tolde,
If he wyll to Houngry
Nedes he muste come us by
To mete with him he wolde.

When Sir Tryamoure discovered himself, the brother giants were furious, and both attacked him. It is useless to follow the details of the combat, but, in the end, both giants were slain, and the knight went on his way. Nor was he too soon, for it was the day appointed when the giant Burlonge was to meet fair Elyne's champion. She, poor lady, was in a state of great anxiety, but she had faith in her lover, and said that if he were alive he would surely come to defend her. At that moment Sir Tryamoure rode up, and held a short parley with Burlonge, as to their mutual willingness to fight. But Elyne, although she saw that a champion had appeared on her part, knew him not until she was told by a herald, and then she knelt in prayer for his success.

The combatants engaged, with the usual prelude of shivered lances ; and, when they betook themselves to their swords, Sir Tryamoure missed a stroke, and lost his weapon. Not being deficient in assurance, he asked that he might have it again, and the giant, with unexampled

generosity, consented, provided he told his name. But
when he heard it—

> Than, sayde Burlonge, thou it was
> That slewe my brother Maradas,
> A fayre happe then befell.
> Syr Tryamoure sayde to hym tho,
> So have I done thy bretherne two
> That on the mountayne dyde dwell.
> Burlonge sayd, Wo may thou be,
> For thou hast slayn my bretherne thre,
> Sorowe hast thou sought ;
> Thy swerde getest thou never agayn
> Tyll I be venged, and thou slayne.

And, so saying, he aimed a mighty stroke at the knight,
but his feet slipped, and he fell. Sir Tryamoure instantly
picked up his sword, and cut off the giant's leg at the
knee, and then tauntingly told him to stand up and continue the fight. This, after being furnished with a fresh
sword, Burlonge did, and, for a time, fought upon his
stumps ; but not for long, for the mighty Tryamoure cut off
his head.

> Now is Burlonge slayne,
> And Tryamoure with mayne
> Into the castell wente
> To that lady that was full bryght ;
> And at the gate she mette the knyght,
> And in her armes she him hente.[1]
> She sayd, Welcome, Syr Tryamoure,
> Ye have bought my love full dere,
> My herte is on you lente.[2]
> Then sayde all the barons bolde,
> Of hym we will our landes holde,
> And thereto they dyd assent.

[1] Held, clasped.   [2] Remains with you.

There is little more to chronicle. They named a speedy day for their marriage, and sent for Queen Margarete. On her arrival, Tryamoure claimed the fulfilment of her promise, that she would tell him who his father was ; which she did, and gave her whole history. Thereupon he wrote to King Aradas to come to Hungary, which he did gladly.

The young folks were married, Sir Tryamoure crowned King of Hungary. King Aradas and Queen Margarete were united, and

> In joye togyder they ledde theyr lyfe
> All theyr dayes withoute stryfe.

The Squyr of lowe degre

The Squyr of lowe Degre.

COPLAND'S version, from which I have taken this Romance, seems to be the only one now known. It was reprinted by Ritson, and may also be found in Warton's " History of English Poetry."

The parentage of this Squire of low degree is not given, but, at the time when this story opens, he had served the King of Hungary, by whom he was much liked, for seven years, and now held the position of Marshal of the Royal Hall. He was good-looking and well made, was liked by all men, and could hold his own in the lists; but he nourished a secret grief, and was ever mourning, but no man wist why.

The fact was, he was deeply in love with the daughter of his master the king, and, being a gentleman in feeling, could confide his secret to no man, so he went about moping, and "ever he sayde wayle a waye." In this desperate condition of mind, he wandered one day into the

14

garden, and, as delineations of home life are very scarce in these Romances, perhaps I may be pardoned for introducing a description of this place.

And in the garden, as I wene,
Was an arber fayre and grene ;
And in the arber was a tre,
A fayrer in the world might none be.
The tre it was of Cypresse,[1]
The fyrst tre that Jesu chose,
The sother[2] wood and lykamoure,[3]
The red rose, and the lyly floure,
The box, the beche, and the larel tre,
The date, also the damyse ;[4]
The fylbyrdes[5] hangyng to the ground,
The fygge tre and the maple round ;
And other trees there was mane one,
The pyany,[6] the popler, and the plane,
With brode braunches all aboute,
Within the arber, and eke withoute.
On every braunche sate byrdes thre,
Syngynge with great melody.
The lavorocke[7] and the nightyngale,
The ruddocke,[8] the woodwele,[9]
The pee,[10] and the Popinjaye,[11]
The thrustle[12] saynge both nyght and daye ;
The marlyn[13] and the wrenne also,
The swalowe whypping to and fro ;
The jaye jangled them amonge,
The larke began that mery songe ;
The sparowe spredde her on her spraye,
The mavys[14] songe with notes full gaye ;

[1] The cross is said to have been made of three woods, of which Cypress. was one.

[2] Sothernwood.   [3] Sycamore.   [4] Damson.   [5] Filberts.   [6] Peony.
[7] Lark.   [8] Redbreast.   [9] Woodpecker. [10] Pie.   [11] Parrot.
[12] Thrush.   [13] The merlin hawk.   [14] The singing thrush.

The nuthake [1] with her notes newe,
The sterlynge set her notes full trewe ;
The goldfynche made full mery chere
When she was bente upon a brere ; [2]
And many other foules mo,
The osyll [3] and the thrush also.

Into this arbour went the love-lorn Squire to mourn his sad fate, and, presuming there were no eavesdroppers, he made his plaint aloud. But it happened that this bower was underneath the window of the princess's apartment, and

In her oryal [4] there she was,
Closed well with royall glas,
Fulfylled it was with ymagery.

She opened the window, and there she saw the Squire lying on the ground making his moan—how that he loved her dearly, but, because of his poverty and position, might never hope to wed her. So she spoke to him, asking him why he was so mournful, and why he always went about so sadly, promising that whatever he told her should be held as strictly confidential. Here was an opportunity, and he did not neglect it. He dropped on one knee, and poured forth his tale of passionate love—how that, for seven years, she had been the object of his humble adoration, and that if she did not give him a word of comfort, he must needs go away, and become a hermit.

The lady listened to his tale, and told him that she

[1] Nuthatch.   [2] Briar.   [3] Ousel, or blackbird.
[4] Here the word probably means a turret.

reciprocated his affection; but that no one must know of it, more especially the steward, or it would be certain death to him. She bade him shake off his melancholy, abandon all idea of turning hermit, but to go forth and do man's work in the world. That if he would win her, he must begin with chivalry; that he must go into many countries in search of adventures, and, after fighting three battles, he would be worthy of being knighted. That this mode of life was to last for seven years, when he was to make a pilgrimage to Jerusalem, and then return to Hungary, where, through fame of his deeds, the king would wed him to her; and that during the whole of the seven years she would be true to him. She also would see him properly equipped and horsed, with six yeomen to ride with him; and she would give him a thousand pounds to start with, and more when he required it. The Squire was profuse in his thanks, kissed his lady thrice, and departed.

But the king's steward, Sir Maradose, who was both false and treacherous, overheard their wooing, and vowed to be avenged on that fair lady, with whom he himself was in love—a passion which was not returned by the princess.

Meanwhile, the Squire robed himself to perform his accustomed duties for the last time, serving the king at dinner on his knee. The king fed sumptuously on

Deynty meates that were dere,
With partryche, pecoke and plovere,

With byrdes in bread y-bake,
The tele, the ducke, and the drake,
The cocke, the curlewe, and the crane ;
With fesauntes fayre there were no want,
Both storkes and snytes, there were also,
And venyson freshe of bucke and do.

The king, however, ate nought, but gazed curiously and thoughtfully upon his Squire, thinking of the singular tale Sir Maradose, his steward, had told him—of what he had overheard, with the addition of a criminal liaison between the Squire and the Princess. The king had not believed the story, and had told his steward that if his daughter loved the Squire, and he could prove himself worthy of her, he saw no objection to their union ; and that, if he found that the steward had defamed them for envy's sake, he would imprison him for twelve years, and then hang him.

The steward had asseverated the truth of his story, and added, that if the king would but give him a sufficient force of men, he would take the Squire that night, in his daughter's chamber. The king had still disbelieved Sir Maradose, but promised him thirty men at arms, on condition, that if the Squire did not enter the lady's chamber, he was not to be touched, nor even if he kissed her, "so that it be done courteously ;" but only, if he came with a company "for to betraye that fayre ladye," then was he to be seized, and brought to the king's presence.

These thoughts, then, were in the king's mind as he looked upon his Squire, whom he trusted and loved, and he was not surprised when, after dinner, the Squire waited on him, and, on bended knee, asked him—

> As ye are lorde of chyvalry,
> Give me leve to passe the sea
> To prove my strengthe with my ryght hande
> On Godes enemyes in uncouth land.
> And to be knowe in chyvalry
> In Gascoyne, Spayne and Lumbardy ;
> In eche batayle for to fyght
> To be proved a venterous knyght.
> The kyng said to the squyer tho
> Thou shalt have good leve to go,
> I shall the gyve both golde and fe
> And strength of men to wende with thee,
> If thou be true in worde and dede,
> I shall the helpe in all thy nede.

He let no grass grow under his feet, for he collected his men and set forth at once ; but he had scarcely ridden over a mile, when they came to a village, and there he proposed that they should sup, and stay the night. But, at supper, he remembered that he had not bidden the princess farewell, so he started off alone to do this act of courtesy. He entered the castle, and went straight to his lady's chamber, not witting that Sir Maradose, and his force, were lying in wait for him close by. He knocked at her door, and conjured her to open it, but she, wrapping herself in a mantle of cloth of gold, " she sayd, go away thou wicked wyght," and utterly refused to open the door ; but when

> I am your owne squyr, he said,
> For me lady be not dysmayde,

> Come I am full pryvely
> To take my leave of you, lady ;

then she let him in, premising that it was only in order to "give him kysses thre, and a thousande pounde unto your fe," begging him to go forth, and be an adventurous knight. Whilst they were thus speaking, his enemies were approaching, and all set on him at once ; but he slew seven of them, and also the villain steward, before he was overpowered. His captors stripped him of his garments, in which they arrayed the dead steward, whose features they gashed, so as to be unrecognizable, and deposited outside the princess's door. They bore him, unhurt, before the king, who, telling him that as he wished to be his son, he would take care of him for seven years ; and so sent him to prison.

When the princess saw the dead body, which she imagined to be that of her lover, she made a great moan.

> And in her armes she toke hym there,
> Into the chamber she dyd hym bere ;
> His bowels soon she dyd outdrawe,
> And buryed them in Godde's lawe ;
> She sered [1] that body with specery,
> With vyrgin wax and commendry,[2]
> And closed him in a maser [3] tre,
> And set on hym lockes thre ;
> She put him in a marble stone
> With quanyt gynnes [4] many one,

[1] Embalmed—wrapped it in a case, or waxed cloth.
[2] Commendationes, or offices for the dead.
[3] A hard-wood tree. Wooden bowls were termed maser bowls.
  Fastenings.

And set hym at hir beddes head,
And every day she kyst that dead.
Soone at morne when she up rose
Unto that dead body she gose,
Therfore wold she knele downe on her kne
And make her prayer to the trynite,
And kysse that body twyse or thryse
And fall in a swowne or she myght ryse.
Whan she had so done,
To churche then wolde she gone,
Than wolde she here masses fyve
And offer to them whyle she myght lyve ;
There none shall knowe but heven kynge
For whom that I make myne offrynge.

The king could but notice his daughter's sadness, and
spoke to her about it in a most kindly and fatherly way ;
asking her the reason why she, who was wont to be the
merriest of all the court, was now so sad, and also why
she, who used to be decked according to her rank, now
went about in mourning weeds ; and he promised to gratify
her every taste, if she would but rouse herself and shake
off the melancholy that oppressed her : but all he could
get from her was—

Gramercy, father, so mote I the,
For all these thynges lyketh not me.
Unto her chamber she is gone
And fell in sowning sore anone,
With much sorow and sighing sore,
Yet seven yeare she kept hym there.

The Squire was, as we have seen, put in prison, but the
king soon came to hear of the truth, and went to him
privily, and, bidding him to keep his counsel, told him he

was free, and might go across the sea as originally intended, and that when his journeying should be done, he was to come to the king's chamber ; and the king, being fully satisfied of his Squire's innocence, promised that he should have his daughter's hand and be his successor.   Moreover, the king supplied him with ample funds, and the Squire went forth " full mery " ; but none knew of it save himself and the king.   He made himself famous by his deeds of arms in Tuscany, Lombardy, and Portugal ; and then, the seven years having expired, he went to Jerusalem, made his offerings there, and returned to Hungary.   When he detailed his adventures, the king was delighted, and welcomed him warmly, charging him, however, to

> Let none wete of my menne [1]
> That out of prison thou shouldest be,
> But in my chamber holde the styll
> And I shall wete my doughter's wyll.

So he went to see his daughter, but, passing under her window, he heard her complaining ; and, as he stopped and listened, thus he heard her addressing the supposed body of her beloved Squire—

> Alas, then sayd that lady dere,
> I have the kept this seven yere,
> And now ye be in powder small,
> I may no longer holde you withall.
> My love, to the earth I shall the bring,
> And preestes for you to reade and synge.
> Yf any man aske me what I have here,
> I will say it is my treasure ;

[1] Let none of my household know.

> If any man aske why I do so,
> For no theves shall come thereto.
> And, squyer, for the love of thee
> Fy on this worldes vanyte ;
> Farewell golde, pure and fyne,
> Farewell velvet and satyne ;
> Farewell castelles and maners also,
> Farewell huntynge and hawkynge to ;
> Farewell all revell, myrthe, and play,
> Farewell pleasure and garmentes gay ;
> Farewell perle and precyous stone,
> Farewell my juilles everych one ;
> Farewell mantell and scarlet red,
> Farewell crowne unto my head ;
> Farewell hawkes and farewell hounde,
> Farewell markes and many a pounde ;
> Farewell huntynge at the hare,
> Farewell harte and hynde for evermare.
> Now will I take the mantell and ye rynge,
> And become an ancresse [1] in my lyuynge.

But her father spoke to her, and told her she must think of no such things, but put off her mourning, for she must wed a knight ; but this she utterly refused for any consideration on earth. Then her father told her all—how that she had been weeping over, and bewailing the body of the treacherous steward, Sir Maradose. She very gently upbraided him.

> Alas, father, anone she sayde,
> Why hath this traytour me betraid ?
> Alas, she sayd, I have great wrong
> That I have kept him here so long.
> Alas, father, why dyye [2] so,
> Ye might have warned me of my fo ;

---

[1] Anchoresse—a female Anchorite or Hermit.   [2] Do ye.

> And ye had told me who it had be,
> My love had never been dead for me.

So saying she fainted, and her father, when she had come
to, told her that her love was alive, and in the castle.
Naturally, she was eager to see him, and she was soon
gratified. The meeting can be better imagined than
described. The Squire was made knight and lord, and

> Ther was myrth and melody,
> With harpe, getron,[1] and sautry,
> With rote,[2] ribible,[3] and clockarde,[4]
> With pypes, organs, and bumbarde ;
> With other mynstrelles them amonge,
> With sytolphe[5] and with sautry songe,
> With fidle, recorda,[6] and dowcemere,[7]
> With trompette and with claryon clere,
> And dulcet pipes of many cordes.

The wedding was soon arranged. All the nobility of
Hungary were bidden to come to it, and the revels
consequent on it lasted forty days : after which, the king
led the quondam squire into the midst of his barons, and
then and there abdicated in his favour ; and, afterwards

> That yong man and ye quene his wyfe,
> With joy and blysse they led theyr lyfe.

[1] Cithern or zithern.
[2] Rote—a sort of cymbal.
[3] Ribible—a kind of fiddle.
[4] Probably hand bells.
[5] A small psalterium with strings placed over a sound board.
[6] A kind of flageolet.
[7] Dulcimer.

The Knight of the
Swanne.

The Knight of the Swanne.

THIS very pretty Romance is somewhat general. According to Sir Francis Palgrave, the oldest form in which it appears, is in the "Chronicle of Tongres" by the *Maitre de Guise*. It is incorporated in the German Romance of "Lohengrin," and there is even an Icelandic Saga of Helis the Knight of the Swan, wherein Julius Cæsar is said to be his father.

In the British Museum are two MSS. of this Romance, both of fifteenth century, one on vellum and one on paper. Ames says there was a copy printed on parchment by Wynkyn de Worde, 1512; but I have taken mine from one printed by Copland, in the British Museum, which is believed to be unique, and which was translated by the order of Edward Duke of Buckingham (beheaded on Tower Hill, 17th May, 1521), who claimed to be lineally descended from Helyas.

In the kingdom of Lilefort, or Strong Island, reigned a

king named Pieron, who had to wife the Princess
Matabrune, the daughter of a neighbouring king, who had
been constantly at war with the kingdom of Lilefort ; and,
by this marriage, the feud was healed. This couple had
but one son, named Oriant, and he grew up to be a most
discreet and able prince, succeeding to his father's throne
on his decease.

Fond of all manly sports, he indulged in the princely
pastime of hunting, and, one day, his greyhounds started a
great hart, which led them a long chase, gaining safety at
last, and escaping the king and his hounds, by leaping into
the river. The king gave up all idea of pursuit, and
returned homewards; but, feeling hot and tired, he dismounted by the side of a fountain, and having tied his
horse to a tree, sat himself down to rest.

He had not been there long, when " there came to him
a yonge damoysel, moche grevous and of noble maintene,
named Beatrice, accompanied of a noble knight and two
squires, with iiii damoyselles, the which she held in her
service and famyliarite." This lady held all the lands
thereabouts in signorie from King Oriant, but had never
yet seen her feudal superior : so she began their interview
with reproving the stranger for hunting on her ground,
telling him that, even if he had taken the hart, he should
not have kept it, and that he should make her some
recompense before he should be allowed to depart. The
king, who was so smitten by her charms that he fell

desperately in love with her at first sight, replied very graciously to her, saying that he would not knowingly have done anything to give her displeasure, and that, if he thought he had done her any damage, even to the extent of a farthing, he would recompense her ; but that as he was King Oriant, and she merely held under him, he thought he had a fair right to hunt on his own land.

When they heard who the stranger huntsman was, the knight, who was with the lady Beatrice, kneeled down, and did obeisance for her to the king, begging his pardon, because she knew him not. " Then answered the kynge to him and said, Know ye, noble knight, that I accept ynoughe the excuse that ye have made for your noble lady. But she shall make me amendes in suche maner as shal be

15

agreeable, for the beaute and formosite of her noble persone moveth me to be her husbande, and to take her to wife and spouse, the which is my whole desire."

But, autocratic as was the monarch, he did not think that the mere expression of his wish was sufficient for the lady, and, therefore, he commenced to woo her, in a style somewhat differing from the love-making of this nineteenth century, but so quaint and curious, and presenting such a picture of the courteous manners of that time, that even at the risk of being somewhat wearisome, I give the brief courtship *in extenso.*

" Than the king began for to speake in this maner, and sayd, Gentil damoysell, pleasaunt, vertuous, garnished of al beaute, in whome I have totali set the love of my herte, is it not wel your wil that I be your husband. Pleaseth it you not to be my wife to th'ende that I make you to be crowned as quene and lady of Lilefort. May ye finde in your hert by suche maner to accomplishe my wil, that you and I might be assembled and conjonct by marriage. Answere ye nowe and say your advise.

" Ha sir, saide she right humblye, I am not digne[1] ne suffisaunt that ye do to me suche honour, for the hand-maiden or subjecte ought not, ne maye not, in any thynge compare to her prence and lorde. But sitte it pleaseth you to commaund me so to doo, in disparsinge to me of your grace, I wer right simple and evil instruct if I refused

[1] Worthy.

your pleasure, and the excellent honour that ye so benignely and of your goodnesse unto me present. For if it should please you to marry me to the least knight of your noble company, yet ought I to consent of right. Wherfore to you that is my lorde, and to other incomparable, I am all redy to obey and accept your good and

noble wil in the honour wherto ye require me, the which with good hert I ottroye ¹ and graunt you.

" And than King Oriant tooke her by the hande and said, Certes lady I promise you on the faith of knighthood, that as long as ye be on live ² never to espouse any other woman than you, and I assure you even here that I shal be your husbande.

" And thus bi a comin accorde, and by the consentement

¹ Utter, to give.   ² Alive.

of them bothe, was promised the saide mariage with one
cordiall love."

The king, at once, took her with him to Lilefort, riding
along together, in pleasant companionship, in that sweet
May-tide. Arrived at the palace, his first care was to
introduce his fair betrothed to his mother, and begged of her
to treat her kindly. For there was a look in Matabrune's
face, the reverse of welcome to the bride, and she plainly
told the king that such a match was beneath his dignity,
when he might ask the hand of the richest and most noble
princess on earth. But he gave her plainly to understand
that it was his will and determination, and the crafty old
queen consented with her lips, but in her heart she hated
the fair Beatrice.

Next day the marriage was celebrated with great
solemnity, and the feasting and merrymaking was continued
for many days, but the chronicler relates of the dowager
queen : "And yf she made ani chere at the said feast it
was bi false semblant and manere of doinge, for unjustly
and wrongfully she conspired alway some evil upon the
noble quene Beatrice."

The king loved his bride so dearly that he attended not
sufficiently to the affairs of his kingdom, a fact of which
his enemies took speedy cognizance ; and things came to
such a pass, that he was compelled to abandon his life of
enervating uxoriousness, buckle on his arms, and take the
field against his foes. It was a hard task to part from his

dear wife, but he left her, as he thought, in good hands, for he had given his mother, Queen Matabrune, strict charge respecting her, and she had promised to treat her as her daughter, and better than herself: but her " wordes were not accordaunt to her dedes, for they were al but abuse and false simulacion."

The queen was *enceinte*, and the wicked old woman took occasion of her condition to wreak her spite and malice upon her. She interviewed the midwife that would be in attendance upon Beatrice, and promised to richly reward her, as well as provide for her family, if she would only follow out the instructions she would give her. The *sage-femme*, dazzled by the bait, promised compliance, and a most villainous plot was hatched by these two worthies. At her confinement the queen bore six sons and one daughter, each of whom came into the world with a silver collar or chain around its neck; and, whilst the young queen was unconscious, the children were taken away by the cruel mother-in-law, who substituted in their stead seven new-born puppies.[1]

When the queen recovered her senses, she heard Matabrune and the midwife talking of this strange occurrence, and, when she asked to see her child, they showed her the seven puppies, upbraiding her with the unnatural birth. The queen, amazed, and unable to contradict their assertions, found a refuge in sobbing and weeping, thinking it a direct visitation from God for some

[1] See next page.

sin she had committed, and hoping that it might be
condoned by her leading the remainder of her life in some
convent, in religious exercises and penances. The false old
queen tried to comfort her by the assurance that the king
should never know of it, determining, all the time, to tell
him as soon as he returned home.

The next thing Matabrune had to do, was to get rid of

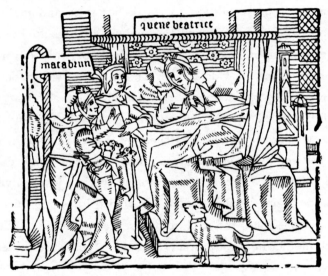

the seven children, and to this end she called to her her
secretary Markes, and, first reminding him that he owed all
his fortunes to her, told him that therefore it behoved him
to do her bidding. Markes replied that it was but his
duty to do whatever she commanded, and the wily old
dame then told him that the queen had borne seven
children, all of whom came into the world with silver chains

about their necks, and that this was something so abnormal, that she, fearing they might become murderers and thieves, thought they ought to be drowned, or killed, at once, rather than grow up and do evil ; adding, that she had persuaded the queen that she had given birth to seven puppies. Markes, of course, undertook the commission, and promised that nothing should ever be heard of the babes.

He mounted his horse, having the little ones wrapped in his mantle, rode about ten miles from the city, and entered a forest, when he thought he would dismount and see how the children fared. They were fair to look upon, and, as he thought upon them, he considered that as they had made their appearance into the world wearing those collars, perhaps God had ordained them to come to wealth and honour ; and, when the babes laughed and crowed to him, he could no longer steel his heart to drown or kill them, but determined to adopt a middle course by abandoning them to their fate, trusting to Providence to protect them. And thus he addressed them : " Alas, poore chyldren, it greveth me sore for to leve you here in this place as desolate, wandred and habandoned of your blode. But I hope that He that hath willed to creat and fourme you to your good mothers body, wil not leve you dispurveyed, and fare ye wel, to God I commaunde you, children, for I shal se you nevermore. And thus amyably took the said Markes leve of the ḃíí litle children, the which, at his departing, took theym in his armes and

pitiousli kissed them in weping tenderly with salte teres.'
He then returned, and told Matabrune that he had hewed
them in pieces, and cast them into the river.

Meanwhile, the babes were in somewhat evil case,
" dolorouslye wayling, and as all dead for honger," when

providentially, a hermit named Helias, who lived in the
forest, passed by that way, and, weeping with pity and
compassion, he bore them to his little hermitage, and there
warmed them and fed them as best he could. But the care
of such a family not coming within the scope of the general

daily life of hermits, he prayed for Divine help in this, to
him, novel situation ; and, incontinently, his prayer was
heard, " for miraculously there came into his house a fayre
white goat, the wiche benignely came nere to the ꝟíí little
children in presenting to them her milke, and ther she gave
them sucke naturally as their nource. . . . And thus this
white goate gave milke sufficiently to them, and than
retourned to the wood. And so longe she gave them souke
that they began to gro and waxe somewhat stronge, and
folowed her in the woude and about the hermitage."

" Whan the forsaid children were come to age of
puerilete the devoute hermite Helyas made and appropryed
to eche of them a cote of leves of the trees, or of suche as
he coulde get. And so they were playing within the
forest, where as thei gathered fruite to eate with theyr
bread, for in that pointe were they nourished under the
grace of God, and by the dylygence of the good hermete,
which with good herte administred the bread of the
almesses [1] given him."

King Oriant returned home victorious over his enemies,
and Matabrune, accompanied by the midwife, went to meet
him. She told her tale, with artful embellishments, and
the midwife corroborated all she said, so that the king
must needs believe them ; and he grieved sorely, so that
when he was come to his palace " he was so inwardli dis-
comforted that he laide him on a bedde, where as he fell

[1] Alms.

on slepe for sorow and melancoly." Beatrice, who, on her
side, was also deeply sorrowing, was informed by a squire
of what her mother-in-law had done ; and, knowing that it
was of no use to welcome her husband home, she spent
her time in praying to the Virgin for strength and assistance in this her time of trial.

The king assembled his council, to inform them of his
grief, and to ask their opinion as to what should be done
to the queen. The bishop spoke first, and his advice was
that she should be kept in honourable durance, and be
judged by God, by which means the truth would ultimately
be made manifest. A knight then expressed his opinion
that she should be burnt; but this was utterly repugnant to
the king's feelings, and he agreed with the bishop. And
it was so settled, that she should be kept under the super-
vision of two knights, and treated well in every respect.
For this treatment she was very thankful, and spent her
time in religious exercises.

Meanwhile how did the children fare? The good hermit
baptized them, and they roamed freely in the forest, bare-
legged and footed, clad only in their little coats of green
leaves. Then it came to pass that a Yeoman of the Hunt,
named Savary, was hunting in the forest, when he came
upon seven children, each with a silver chain round its
neck, gathering wild apples, which they ate with bread.
He spoke to them, but they stared at him and ran away ;
he pursued them until they took refuge in the hermitage,

when the old hermit appeared, and begged of him to do them no harm. Savary was naturally curious, and, in answer to his questions, he told him the children's history, as far as he knew it.

The huntsman guessed who they were, and, on his return, informed Matabrune of what he had seen. She, too, recognized the situation, and sent for Markes ; and, full of madness and fury, " put out his eyen, and handled him so that many wened [1] that he had been dead." She thought she had a more unscrupulous tool in the huntsman, and therefore she commanded him to go into the forest and slay the children, promising him great reward.

He set out with six companions, but on their way they saw a great crowd, and, asking what occasioned it, were informed that a woman was to be burnt for killing her child. This set Savary a-thinking, and he repented him of the errand on which he was bound: so he spoke to his companions, asking them, if burning to death was the fitting punishment for a woman killing her child, which, after all, was her own, what ought to be done to them, who were about to kill seven innocent children in whom they had no personal interest ? He therefore suggested that they should do them no harm, but only take their silver collars from them ; to which his companions agreed.

So they journeyed until they came to the hermitage, where they found but six of the children—the seventh, who

[1] Thought.

was godson to the hermit, having accompanied him on a begging expedition to the neighbouring villages. The children cried when they beheld these strange men, who, whilst bidding them fear nothing, were busy in taking the collars from their necks; but, no sooner were they deprived of these ornaments, than they were changed into white swans, which flew away, "making a piteous and lamentable

crye." The men were terribly frightened at the conse-quences of their act, but determined to return to Mata-brune with six collars, and tell her they had lost the seventh by the way. She was very mad at not having them all, but eventually grew appeased, and sent for a goldsmith, commanding him to make a cup of the chains.

But these were no ordinary chains of silver, and, when

the goldsmith melted one in a crucible, to his utter astonishment it yielded sufficient silver to make two cups of the required weight. These he made, kept one himself, took the other to Matabrune, who was satisfied with the weight of metal she got; and gave the other five chains to his wife for safe keeping, rightly believing there was something weird and uncanny about them.

On the return of the hermit Helias and his godson they found the hermitage empty, and sought the children far and near with diligent search and shouting, but without avail; and a miserable night they spent, on the morrow continuing their quest, with the same result. One thing, however, the young Helias found, and knew not that they were his brethren ; on a fair pond he beheld six white swans, which when he approached them, came towards him, took the bread he gave them, and allowed him to stroke their feathers as he would. And every day he went to the pond to feed and caress them ; but nought could he nor the hermit ever find of the lost children. And so, in this simple manner the young Helias grew up to man's estate, strong, healthy, and vigorous, unversed in the ways of the world, religious and simple-minded enough for a priest, for which his foster father intended him, until his purpose was altered by an angelic vision.

Think not that the wicked Matabrune was quiet all this time. Far from it, she only bided until she could find a subservient tool, and this took sixteen years to find. It

irked her that Beatrice should be alive, and nothing should
thwart her purpose of compassing her death. At length
she found some one fitted to her purpose, " a knight disloial
and wicked named Makaire," who was quite willing to
bear false witness against Beatrice, which witness he was
willing to defend with his body. The king would fain
have let the matter rest, but could not, for here was a knight
who would affirm, at the expense of his life, that what he
said was true, and would not be gainsaid. Of course the
queen could appear by her champion, and do battle with
him ; but none came forward, and she could but pray to
God for deliverance, and trust to His goodness.

In the meantime Helias the hermit had an angelic
vision, in which the whole story of the seven children and
Queen Beatrice was related to him, as also the fact that
the swans were the lost ones, who should some day be
restored to their proper shapes. The angel also told him
that his godson was to go to his father's court, to be his
mother's champion, never doubting that he would be victorious over the wicked Makaire. He further prophesied,
that from Helias the younger should spring the famous
Godfrey de Bouillon who should conquer the Holy Land.
At his awakening he called the youth, told him the whole
vision, and bad him set forth in aid of his mother. This
he did, clothed but in leaves, barefoot, and with a simple
staff in his hand ; but, in bidding his foster father farewell,
he begged him to feed his brethren, the swans, diligently.

Arrangements were being made for the queen's death when he arrived at Lilefort, and the porters would not admit him into the precincts of the court, because of his peculiar dress and appearance ; but at last some one told him where Makaire was, and led him before the Consistory, where were the king, the accused queen, all the nobility, and the foul villain Makaire. The king thought he was a madman, but a knight said he had heard him speak sense ; and, on the king asking him his business, he replied that he sought Makaire. On being shown him he at once strode to him, and, defying him, he smote him such a blow with his fist that he felled him to the earth, and, at his rising, he was fain to retire from the royal presence covered with blood.

The king questioned him why he had so treated Makaire, and he replied that he had come thither by God's command to be his mother's champion, but before he would say more he would embrace her ; and, to the marvel of all, he went up to, and kissed and embraced the queen. He then told all his story, and the king asked the queen whether the substitution of the puppies for the children was true ; but she replied that at the time she was unconscious, and, of course, knew nothing about it.

The king, however, believed the story, and, instead of sending his queen back to prison, had her led to rich apartments; but he cast Makaire into prison, to be kept in safe custody until the day of battle. He also gave orders

for the making of rich armour for his son Helias, and then,
in order to make assurance doubly sure, he visited the
hermit, who thoroughly convinced him of the truth of his
son's story.   On his return, his first act was to restore his
injured queen to all liberty, for which she humbly praised

and thanked God : but Matabrune was put in durance under
the safe keeping of four sergeants.

The day for the combat had come, and Helias was
armed as befits a king's son, whilst the caitiff Makaire
must have seen that his fate was sealed, when he found
the queen at liberty, and such a champion to fight for her.

Still he swore that he had "good cause in that quarel different that the one against the other wolde sustaine." Of course the combat was gained by Helias, who, when about to despatch Makaire, was entreated by the latter to spare his life for an hour, and he would reveal all Matabrune's treason, and tell the name of the goldsmith who made the silver cup for her. Helias would fain have killed the traitor then and there, but could not resist the temptation of hearing the false knave confess his misdeeds, so he respited him. Brought before the king, he made a full confession, and then, " bi the commaundement of the noble Kynge Oriant, the sayd fals reproved traytre Makayre was drawen to the galowes, and there shamfully hanged and strangled as a recreant knight that he was."

Their return to the palace was signalized by exuberance of joy and festivity, not forgetting masses in thanksgiving. The goldsmith was sent for, and brought with him the extra cup and the five chains. " Than the kyng and the queene tooke those precious chaynes and kissed them reverentlie in weeping, and bewayling naturally theyr poore children that by so great a treason were mued [1] and converted into swannes." The eyeless Markes was then brought forward, and told the part he had taken in Matabrune's villainy; but when Helias heard him he was moved with pity, and praying to God to have mercy on that poor blind man, and restore to him his sight, he made the sign

[1] Changed.

16

of the cross over Markes's eyes, and he saw as clearly as ever he did. But, whilst all this was going on, Matabrune managed to make her gaolers drunk, and escaped, withdrawing, with certain of her friends, to her castle of Maubruiant, a fact which the king lamented, and vented his wrath on those who had her in keeping.

Among all the joy, there yet remained the fact that the other children were still swans; and Helias, having asked of, and obtained from, his father the five chains and the cup, declared that he would not rest until he had transformed them. Nor had he long to wait, for lo! before the king's palace, in the river which ran there, swam six noble swans. The king, queen, and Helias descended to the river bank, and when the swans saw Helias approach the brink "they came lightli fawning and flikering about him, making him chere, and he playned lovingli theyr fethers." [1] But when he put the chains about their necks they were miraculously transformed into four young men and one maiden, to the great joy of the king and queen, who kissed them, and could scarce contain themselves for joy.

"And when the other swanne (whose chaine was molten for to make the cuppes as afore is sayd) saw his brethren and his sister retourned into theyr humaine fourmes he lept agayne all sorowfully into the river, and for dole that he had, he plucked almost al his fethers to the bare flesshe. And whan the good Helias saw him so dolorously demeane

---

[1] Played lovingly with their feathers.

himselfe, he took him to weepe for sorow, and recomforted
him, sayinge, My dere brother, my frende, have somwhat
pacience, and discomforte you not. For I shall make so
meeke and humble praiers unto God Almighti for you,
that yet I shall se you ones a noble knight. And than the
swanne began to enclyne and bowe downe his head, as in
thanking him, and syth plunged himselfe all togyther in
the water."

The king and queen sorrowed a while, but they had five
living children to console them, and Helias bade them be
of good cheer, for in all probability the sixth would soon
be restored to them, in his own proper shape. The transformed were taken to church to be re-baptized, and the girl
was christened Rose.

Now King Oriant, perceiving that Helias was beloved
both of God and man, thought that he was fitting to suc-
ceed him, and, calling together all his knights and barons,
he solemnly gave up his kingdom to him, telling him to
do whatever he thought right to his mother Matabrune.
Helias willingly undertook the task of punishing his grandmother, and set out with a mixed force of six thousand
men to besiege the castle of Maubruiant. To take it was
no easy task, but the garrison at length yielded, and
Matabrune was once more a prisoner. "And as soone as
the kinge apperceyved her he came to her with great
courage and kest her to the earth, saying, Ha, false olde
witche, thou hast betrayed my mother, and made us to

suffre muche evyll. Yf it were not for the honour of God and the bloud wherof I am comen, myselfe should slea thee." She begged to be taken before King Oriant, but Helias explained that he had come to do justice upon her; and then, when she found that his determination was fixed, she confessed her sins, and acknowledged that she ought to die. Her shrift was a short one, for " than was wood and dry thornes layd about her, and fyre set therein, and so she was brent for her demerites before al the people."

Then Helias returned, and told his news, which seems to have been received in the most matter-of-fact way. He went and told his mother what he had done, sayinge, Mother, rejoyce you, for ye be revenged now of the perverce Matabrune, for I have made her to be brente for her demerites. And the quene answered, My right dere sonne, I thanke you. Jesus forgeve her soule."

The time passed quietly and uneventfully, until one day, Helias, looking towards the river, saw a swan guiding a ship, which it led to a wharf, and then stopped. Helias found no difficulty in recognizing in the bird his untransformed brother, and knew at once, that it had come to lead him to some place, he knew not whither, where he ought to go. He immediately gave back his kingdom to King Oriant, who gave him a horn of such virtue, that whoever blew it should receive no hurt, and, embarking on board the ship, set off on his unknown voyage.

Here, in order to make the story plain, is a slight

digression, which treats of how Otto the First, Emperor of Almayne or Germany, held court at Nimaye, and the Earl of Frankebourke came before him to accuse the Duchesse of Boulyon of having poisoned his brother, her husband ; and he also alleged that her daughter was illegitimate, and that, therefore, he laid claim to the duchy as being next heir of his father, and, as was usual in those days, he was ready to back his opinion with his life, in single combat with a champion on behalf of the duchess ; but none came forward.

The swan guided Helias to Nimaye, and he, having sounded his horn, which caused all hearers to marvel, disembarked, and the swan and ship disappeared. He introduced himself to the emperor as a knight in search of adventures, and Otto told him that if such was his quest, there was one waiting for him, namely, to defend the Duchesse of Boulyon. He told him her story, and Helias asked for an interview, from which he came, determined to be her champion. A day was fixed, and the fight took place. Helias of course was the victor, and, in spite of the Earl's prayer for mercy, his head was smitten off.

In those days events succeeded each other rapidly, for no sooner had Helias slain the Earl, than, after he had saluted the emperor, he "tooke the duchesses doughter bi the hand, and embraced her, and kissed her benignely in saying, Mi love, ye ought wel to be mi wife, for I have frelie bought you, and saved your honour in champ [1] of batayle.   And the mayden answered humbly, Certainly, noble knyght, my mother and I ben beholden to God and you of the right happy jurney [2] that this daye we have by you receyved ; wherfore, at the good pleasure of mi mother, I yelde me totalli to you, as it hath been promised."

This was all their wooing ; and the next day they were married (the festivities lasting fifteen days), and the duchess resigned her lands and duchy, and, with the consent of the emperor, transferred them to Helias, whilst she retired to a convent.   The young pair set out for their dominions, where they were received with great joy.   Here they abode for seven years in great peace, the young duchess bearing a daughter, who was christened Ydain, who in after years was the mother of Godfrey de Boulogne, and his brothers Baldwin and Eustace.

One day, in sport, his wife asked Helias of what country he was, and what friends he had ; but he sternly forbad her ever to speak of it, saying, that if she did so, he would at once leave her, and never again live with her.   By inadvertence, or impelled by womanly curiosity, she again asked the question.   Helias was now seriously angry, and told her that he should leave her at once.   He called his knights together, and commanded them that they should escort his wife and daughter to Nimaye, to the Emperor Otto, and that they should guard well the duchy in their

---

[1] Battle-field.   [2] Day's work.

behalf ; and as for himself, the ship, led by a swan, would come for him, and he would depart for ever from them. And so it fell out, the ladies went to Nimaye, and the swan-led ship called for Helias.

His wife arrived first, and complained to Otto of her husband's conduct towards her—but only got reproof from him. Helias came soon after, and, in an interview with the emperor, besought his protection towards his wife and daughter, and begged him to see that the latter married nobly—both of which were promised ; after which he bad his wife and child adieu, and sailed away under the guidance of the swan to Lilefort.

Here he was most heartily welcomed by his parents and brethren, but the joy of the father and mother was dimmed by the recollection that they had one son yet in the likeness of a swan. But the queen had had a dream on the previous night, which she related, and, as it seemed to have been sent divinely, it was followed out in the minutest particulars.

The goldsmith was sent for, and he produced the two cups, which he made into two sacramental chalices. Two altars were appointed, upon each of which a chalice was placed, and a bed was placed between the altars. Helias went to the riverside, and called the swan, which immediately came, and followed him into the church, where it was laid in the bed ; and at the prayer of consecration in the mass, the swan returned to its human form, and, joining his hands, humbly gave thanks to God for His goodness. Then, after he had kissed his parents and brethren, the bells were solemnly rung, and a Te Deum was sung in thankfulness to God. And, afterwards, he was baptized, and had the name of Emery bestowed upon him. So King Oriant and his queen Beatrice recovered all their children, and they lived henceforth devoutly, and in the fear of the Lord.

One would imagine that now Helias would have settled down, but he had his own views on the subject. His foster father, the old hermit, was dead, and King Oriant, in thankfulness for his kindness, and in recognition of Divine mercy, had erected a religious establishment where erst was the humble hermitage ; and thither Helias determined to retire, and spend the remainder of his life in religious exercises. But, first of all, he told all his family of the adventures he had undergone since last he had seen them, and then he took his leave of them and went to the hermitage, where he built a castle exactly like that at Boulogne—and, indeed, called it " Boulyon le restaure," and there he abode.

Meanwhile his wife, although in religious retreat, still thought upon her lord, and sent messengers in all directions in search of him. One of them, a squire named Ponce, was luckiest of them all, for, being at Jerusalem, he got hold of a clue to his old master, which he followed with such success, that at length he arrived at Boulyon le restaure. In due time he made himself known to, and was recognized by, his old master, to whom he told his errand, begging him to return to his wife and daughter. But this Helias declared was impossible, for he was vowed to a religious life ; yet he gave him his signet ring, as a token, by which his wife should know that the squire had spoken with him.

On his return to Nimaye, Ponce detailed the result of

his travels, and, having found out where her husband was, she and her daughter at once set out to visit him. They arrived at Boulyon le restaure, only to find him grievously sick, and, indeed, on his death-bed. The meeting on both sides was most tender, but necessarily painful, for very shortly afterwards Helias died—an event which preyed so much upon his wife, that she died immediately of a broken heart.

After having seen her parents buried in the same tomb, Ydain returned to Boulyon and superintended the education of her sons. "And when in their adolescence they were somewhat comen to the age of strengthe, they began to practyse them in shooting with their bows and arbelstre [1] to playe with the swerde and buckeler, to runne, to just, to play with a pollaxe, and to wrastle," and in due time they were each sent to the Emperor of Almayne to be knighted.

❡ Thus endeth ye life and myraculous hystory of the most noble and illustryous Helyas, Knight of the Swanne.

[1] Arblast or arbelast—a cross-bow.

Valentine and Orson.

THE TWO SONNES OF THE EMPEROUR OF GREECE.

THIS Romance is undoubtedly of French origin, and the British Museum has a fine MS. of it (10 E. IV. Royal). The earliest known printed copy is one by Jac. Maillet, *Lyons*, 1489, and it was a favourite both with the early French and Italian presses. There was a fragment of four leaves only of this Romance found in the binding of an oak-covered book in the library of the Duke of Devonshire at Bolton Abbey, which was printed by Wynkyn de Worde, and is, probably, as old as that by Maillet. I take my copy from one of two books printed by Copland.

Pepin le Bref reigned over France, and his fair and virtuous sister, Bellisant, was given in marriage to Alexander, Emperor of Greece, and went to her home at Constantinople. For some little time all went well, until the High Priest, who also seems to have been Comptroller of the imperial household, became enamoured of her; but his advances being indignantly repulsed by the lady, he traduced her to the emperor, who, believing him, would fain have put her to death, but eventually commuted her punishment to banishment, and bade her go to her brother Pepin, accompanied only by her page Blandiman whom she had brought with her from France. As usual with heroines of Romance, after a little lamentation she accepted the inevitable, and set forth on her journey.

But the wicked High Priest still longed to get her in his power, and, arming himself, went in pursuit of the exiles. Great was the fight between him and the doughty squire, and there is no knowing how it would have ended, if a merchant had not appeared on the scene, who, moved by the fair dame's tears and entreaties, championed her cause and made the High Priest retrace his steps.

After a halt of a few days to cure Blandiman's wounds,

they came to a forest in Orleans, where Queen Bellisant, being taken in childbirth, sent her faithful squire for female assistance ; but during his absence she gave birth to two sons, and then " a fresh misery worse than all the rest that she had endured hapned unto this lady ; for as she

lay upon the earth under yᵉ tree, and her two infants by her, suddenly came to her a huge beare, most horrible to behold, and tooke up one of the infants in her mouth, and with great pace hasted into yᵉ thickest of yᵉ forest. This strange and unlookt for accident frighted the distressed lady to the soule, that she cried out most lamentably,

getting up upon her hands and feet to hasten after the
aforesaid beare, which was quickly got out of her sight.
But, alas! it little avayled her to make any further pursute,
for she never came unto the sight of the child, till by
miracle it was at length disclosed." Still, hoping against
hope, she feebly crawled after the bear, until exhausted
nature gave way, and she lay fainting on the ground.

Now it so happened that King Pepin was, that day, in
the same forest, and, as good luck would have it, he espied
the child, and taking it up, bade an attendant to bear the
foundling to Orleans; which was duly done, a nurse was
provided, and the boy was baptized by the name of
Valentine.

Meanwhile Blandiman returned with the assistance he
had been to seek, but found no Bellisant; in her stead,
however, was her brother Pepin, to whom the faithful squire
related the story of his mistress's wrongs: but he seems
to have omitted to mention her confinement, nor did
Pepin tell him of the child he had found—so that when
Bellisant was eventually found by Blandiman, she only
knew that she had lost both her children.

The Romance leaves all in this state, and tells of the
child carried off by the bear. "The Beare (as you heard
before) that had carryed away one of the Children, all this
while had offered it no violence, but bare it unto her Cave,
which was darke and obscure. In this cave the old Beare
had foure young ones, amongst whom shee layd the Childe

to be devoured ; but marke the chance, and you shall finde
it at laste miraculous, for all this while the young Beares
did it no harme, but with their rough pawes stroaked it
softly. The old Beare perceiving they did not devoure it,
shewed a bearish kind of favour toward it, insomuch that
she kept it, and gave it sucke among her yong ones the
space of one whole yeare. The Child, by reason of the

nutriment it received from the Beare, became rough all
over like a beast, and, as he grew in strength, began to
range up and downe in the woods, and when he met with
other beasts would smite them, and gat such mastery over
them, that they began to shun the place wherein he came,
he was so extreame fierce amongst them : and in this beast-

like estate passed he the tearm of 𝕩𝕧 years, growing up to
such strength that scarce any man or beast in the forest
durst stirre abroad fearing to fall into his hands, least he
should put them to death, and after, eate their flesh, more
like unto a ravenous beast, than any humane creature.
His name was called Orson, because a Beare had been his
nurse, and also became rough like a Beare."

Bellisant and her squire wandered over many countries
until they came to a port in Portugal, where dwelt, in an
invincible castle, a giant named Ferragus. Contrary to
the wont of giants, this one received them with kindness,
and introduced Bellisant to his wife ; and with this friendly
giant she abode many years, during which time the merchant, who had previously taken her part, followed the High
Priest to Constantinople, and there publicly impeached
him with his wrong doing. Of course there was but one
method of proving his accusation, and that was in the lists,
in a combat *à l'outrance ;* and King Pepin, being interested
in the good name of his sister, was invited to witness the
combat. He accordingly went to Constantinople, where
the fight was to take place. Naturally, the traitorous High
Priest was worsted, and confessed his sins, as a punishment
for which he was plunged alive into a cauldron of boiling
oil. Universal joy prevailed at the establishment of the
queen's innocence, and before the monarchs parted " there
was a generall peace concluded on both parties between
them, and a most speedy course taken to send abroad into

all parts of the world to seeke out the distressed Lady Bellisant."

King Pepin returned to Paris, where he found Valentine a comely youth, well versed in all the exercises fitted to his age ; and when Pepin went to besiege Rome, which the Saracens had taken, Valentine went with him as his chief commander. At Rome he jousted with the Admiral of the Saracens, and overthrew him, and, at the assault on the city, he performed such prodigies of valour, that he was mainly instrumental in relieving the city from the presence of the hated infidel after which they returned home to France.

Now, King Pepin had two illegitimate sons, Haufray and Henry, who hated Valentine because he was in such favour with their father, and, when the king bestowed upon him the earldom of Clerimont of Auvergne, their rage knew no bounds, and they determined, by any means, to compass his death. An opportunity soon presented itself, for Orson, with his growing strength, was rapidly developing into a nuisance, and daily complaints, from all sides, of his conduct, came to the king, who called his barons together, and offered a reward of a thousand marks for the body of Orson, dead or alive. None cared to essay the task, and the wicked brothers suggested that Valentine should undertake it. He accepted the challenge, to the great grief of the king, and next day set out on his adventure.

He arrived at the forest, and at nightfall he partook of

some refreshment, tied his horse to a tree, and climbed the same—in which situation he spent the night. With the early dawn came the object of his quest, Orson, whose attention was drawn to Valentine's beautiful horse, which he immediately began to claw with his long nails. The horse resisted, and kicked and plunged ; proceedings which upset Orson's temper, and a regular rough and tumble fight between him and the horse was imminent. Valentine, from his leafy height, seeing the danger that threatened his good steed, called to the wild man, that if he wanted to fight anybody, he would come down and oblige him. It was a terrible fight. Orson was wounded by a stab with a knife, and Valentine was bruised and battered in this unfraternal strife, which only came to an end when both were too exhausted to continue it, and then Valentine thus addressed his brother : " Wild-man, wherefore dost not thou yeeld thyselfe to me ? Heere thou livest like a beast, having no knowledge of humane society. Come thy way with me, and I shall make thee know both thyselfe and others. I will give unto thee food of all sorts, and also cloath thee in apparell fitting humaine shape."

The Chronicler does not state how the wild-man understood this harangue, but he evidently did so, for he " fell down upon his knees, and stretched forth his hands towards his Brother, making unto him a signe to forgive him, and he would commit himself under his command ever after, and with further signes promised that during his life he would assist him both in body and goods." Valentine graciously accepted his submission, but took the precaution to make him walk in front until they were out of the wood, when Valentine bound him with one of his horse's girths, and thus "led the Wild-man with him like a Beast, who never resisted, which was a thing most of all to be wondred at."

His uncouthness created much diversion at court; he ate his food in a savage manner, and drank wine in any quantity. But he was faithful to his conqueror, who had him baptized under the name of Orson—or, as some of the older French romances have it, Ursine, a name which would be more appropriate—and "Valentine taught him manners how he should behave himselfe. And so they both lived quietly in the Court of King Pepin."

But heroes of Romance are restless beings, and not particularly home loving, snatching eagerly at any occasion which might lead to adventure, and one soon offered to Valentine. Duke Savary of Aquitaine sent to King Pepin, desiring his aid against "a false and accursed Pagan (called the Greene Knight) who hath beseidged his Confines, and intendeth to have his Daughter by force of armes against his will." This Green Knight was the brother of Ferragus, the kindly Giant, and was a most redoubtable man of war, before whom none could stand, as he "could not be overcome by any, except he were a King's Son, and such an one as had never sucked the breasts of any Woman."

Here then was a foe worthy of Valentine's sword; he
would overthrow the Paladin and rescue the fair Lady
Fezon—for the Green Knight had promised not to kill
the Duke, or possess himself of his daughter, if, in six
months, a champion could be found who could overcome
him.

Valentine, who had the additional inducement of wan-
dering into foreign parts in order to discover his parents,
applied for, and obtained, leave from Pepin to undertake
this adventure, and, accompanied by Orson, he set out,
much to the discomfort of Eglantine, King Pepin's daughter, who was deeply in love with him.

But Haufray and Henry thought they herein saw an
opportunity of wreaking their hatred to Valentine, and,
with their cousin Grygar and thirty men, laid in ambush
for him in a forest, through which he must needs pass. It
was successful, and, after a brave struggle against over-
whelming odds, in which Orson literally fought with tooth
and nail, Valentine was taken prisoner, and Orson sadly
went to Pepin's Court, where, by signs, he told the tale.
He had the satisfaction of a single combat with Grygar,
whom he overcame, and who confessed his treachery, and
was rewarded by being hanged on the nearest tree. King
Pepin then proceeded with a force to deliver Valentine,
executing summary justice on his captors; after which the
brothers went on their quest of the Green Knight.

On their arrival at Aquitaine, Valentine introduced himself to Duke Savary, told him of their errand, and having spoken with the Lady Fezon, bade her notice Orson, who had undertaken to be her champion, and who was the strongest man in the world. The lady looked on the wildman with eyes of affection, a sentiment which was increased when she afterwards met him at dinner, a meal at which the Green Knight was an uninvited guest. This latter was boasting how he would demolish the Champion on the morrow, when Orson rose from table, and, taking the Green Knight by the waist, laid him across his shoulder as if he were a child, and then, seeing a handy wall, threw him against it with such force that all imagined he was killed. After which he calmly resumed his meal.

Next day, being the day appointed for the combat, all things were ready, and two or three knights who claimed priority, having been overthrown and hanged by the Green Knight, Valentine encountered him, and the fight between them lasted till sunset, ending in a drawn battle, which was to be resumed on the morrow. But when the morning came, he caused Orson to be armed in his armour, and to ride his horse, and thus go and fight the Green Knight. The contest was severe, until Orson disencumbered himself of the armour and dragged his opponent from the saddle, when he cast him to the ground, holding him down until he wrung from him the unwilling confession that he yielded.

Summary vengeance was about to be taken upon the

Green Knight, and he was nearly undergoing the death he had caused so many others to suffer, when Valentine came to his rescue, and granted him his life on condition that he should renounce paganism, and should go to France and tell King Pepin that he had been overcome by Valentine and Orson. To this he agreed, and, out of gratitude, he suggested that the two should go and visit his sister Clerimond, who possessed a magic head of brass, which, like Friar Bacon's, spoke, and was possessed of supernatural knowledge. The Lady Fezon was delighted that her champion had obtained the victory, and, being deeply in love with Orson, they were at once betrothed ; but Orson, by signs, made his affianced bride understand that he would not marry her until he had obtained the power of speech. And Valentine, being warned by an angel in a vision that they should at once go and see Clerimond, took his departure, accompanied by Orson.

Meanwhile Blandiman had been sent by his mistress, who still lived in the Giant Ferragus's Castle, to King Pepin, to find out whether that monarch yet entertained his injurious opinions respecting his sister. Blandiman told the story of the bear taking away one child, and the other being lost while Bellisant was in pursuit of the bear ; and, when he said that this happened on the day in which he met King Pepin in the forest in Orleans, it " strucke the King into such admiration, that he began to recollect his wits, and then presently came into his mind the finding of

Valentine in the Forest, and how by the same Valentine, Orson was conquered in the same wood. Then hee began again to think on the story that Blandimain had tould him, and thereby knew that these were the two babes brought forth by his sister; wherefore he sent for his Queene, and other Ladies, to let them understand what Blandimain had declared, saying, ' My Lords, I have long nourished and brought up in my Court two poore Children ; and now it plainly doth appeare they are Sons to an Emperor, and my neere kinsmen—Valentine, the one whom I founde in the Forest of Orleance, brought forth there by my sister Bellysant, in the time of her exile, and Orson, who was likewise vanquished by Valentine, to be his naturale brother, and both Sons to the Emperour of Greece. At these tydings all the Court was wonderfull joyfull, save only Haufray and Henry, who in outward shew seemed glad, but were in their hearts very sorrowfull, for above all things they desired the death of Valentine."

Pepin made up his mind to proceed to Constantinople, to inform his brother-in-law of the good news; and, accompanied by the Green Knight, who had arrived in Paris, and been graciously received, set out on his journey. On his way he paid a visit to the Pope, who informed him that the Soudan of the Saracens was besieging Constantinople, and that the Emperor of Greece was in sore need of help. An expedition to succour him was soon organized, and Pepin set out at the head of two hundred thousand men, to the assistance of his brother-in-law. There was a terrible battle with the Saracens, who, however, were no match for their opponents, and King Pepin entered Constantinople, but the united forces of the two monarchs were insufficient to compel the Saracens to raise the siege.

The history now turns to the two heroes. They, in the course of travel, came to Clerimond's Castle, but were confronted at the entrance by ten sturdy knights who were always on guard. The fair chatelaine was told that two knights desired admittance, and she gave orders that the gate should be well kept, whilst she interrogated them herself from the window. After seeing a ring which her brother the Green Knight had given Valentine as a token, and having consulted the magic head, she gave orders for their admission. But her seneschal or steward demurred, and would not admit them without a fight—which ended disastrously for him, for Valentine killed him.

Clerimond, who fell in love with Valentine at first sight, admired him still more for slaying her seneschal; and when he gave her her brother's ring, her confidence in him was complete, and they all sat down to dinner, after which meal they proceeded to the chamber wherein was kept the brazen head. On their arrival " they found the Chamber doore guarded on this manner. On the one side a grimme fearefull and ugly shapen Villayne, strong and crooked, armed with a club of yron uppon his neck, which offered to make resistance. On the other side of the chamber dore stood a most fierce Lyon." With little ado Valentine seized the lion, and it became powerless, whilst at the same time Orson attended to the "Villayne," knocked him down, and would have slain him, had not Clerimond interfered. They then entered the chamber, which was full of wonders, the chief being the brazen head, which immediately commenced an oration about their birth and parentage, and ended thus: "'Further, thus much I shall also tell thee, that this thy brother here present shal never have use of his tongue till a thread be cut under the same, and then thou shalt heare him speake plainely. Therefore proceed as thou hast begun, and thou shalt prosper : for my time is at a period, sith thou art come to enter this chamber,' and so bending itselfe towards him in token of reverence, it never after spake more." After this there were tender embracings of the brothers. Clerimond informed Valentine that he was her destined husband, and he at once agreed to marry her, provided she turned Christian, to which she joyfully consented. Orson had his tongue cut, and was enabled to speak, and all were happy.

But this was not destined to last, for Clerimond kept a dwarf named Pacolet, who was an enchanter, and possessed a wooden horse, in whose head was a pin, which would direct the flight of the horse through the air in any direction its rider wished, and by means of this equine balloon he visited Ferragus, and informed him of all his sister's doings. Ferragus, as a good, conscientious pagan, fell into a terrible rage at the idea of his sister marrying a Christian, but he dissembled his anger, and instructed Pacolet to tell his lady that he would come in person to visit her, with a noble troop of knights. Of the sincerity of this message Clerimond had doubts, but she could do nothing, and, in due time, Ferragus, with his fleet, arrived.

It would seem as if the minds of giants were naturally warped, for Ferragus, although, as we have seen, was capable of acts of generosity and benevolence, yet harboured the direst treachery towards his sister and her *fiancé;* and, under pretence of taking Valentine to see his mother, and celebrating their marriage in Portugal, he lured them on board his ship, and when fairly at sea he bound both Valentine and Orson, putting them in irons— a proceeding which so infuriated Clerimond, that she would have thrown herself into the sea had she not been prevented.

On the ship's arrival at Portugal, the brothers were put in a dungeon in Ferragus's Castle, and there Bellisant saw them, and was afterwards told by Clerimond who they were—a story which, of course, ended in loud lamentations of the pair, when they thought of the probable fate of the prisoners. But at this moment the dwarf Pacolet appeared, and comforted the ladies by telling them that he would set them all free that night; and this he accomplished by his magic arts. And then, having seated them on his wooden horse, he speedily deposited them at Clerimond's Castle, from whence they sailed to Aquitaine, and arrived safely at Duke Savary's, where Orson, in order to try Lady Fezon's constancy to him, did not declare his name, but assumed the character of a stranger knight.

When Ferragus learned that the escaped prisoners were at Aquitaine, he was in a furious rage, and, having gathered an army, he laid siege to that city, and in one battle took the Duke prisoner; but Orson and Pacolet penetrated into the camp of the enemy, and, by the enchantments of the latter, released the Duke, who, in gratitude, promised to give Orson his daughter Fezon in marriage. In a subsequent battle Ferragus and his host were defeated, and the siege was raised. Orson declared himself, and was happily married to the Lady Fezon.

It may be remembered that King Pepin and the Emperor of Greece were shut up in Constantinople, besieged by the Saracenic Soudan, and Valentine, having now some leisure, determined to go to their assistance. So Pacolet, mounting Valentine and the Green Knight on his aerial courser, soon brought them in presence of the two monarchs, and was introduced to the Emperor as his son. Pacolet was invaluable, for, Valentine and the Green Knight having been taken prisoners, he not only released them, but he persuaded the Soudan to mount his wooden horse—and hey, presto! they were in the palace of the Grecian Emperor at Constantinople. This poor deluded pagan was immediately hanged on the highest tower, in sight of all his hosts.

The story now takes a totally different turn. A King Trompart, a Saracen, and friend of Ferragus, was enamoured of Clerimond, and was aided by a magician, who performed wonderful enchantments, and robbed Pacolet of his horse, on which he placed Clerimond, and so conveyed her to King Trompart's tent. She did not take her abduction quietly, and when Trompart attempted to kiss her, she smote him on the mouth with her fist; which so enraged him, that he caught her up, and, jumping on Pacolet's horse, flew to India—a journey that cost him dear, for the King of India remembered that Trompart had killed his brother, and at once caused his head to be cut off. He, too, fell desperately in love with Clerimond, but refrained from pressing his suit when she told him she was under a vow not to take a husband for the space of a year, and he entertained her handsomely in his palace.

They mourned her loss in Aquitaine, and Pacolet revenged himself on his rival magician by killing him; he also brought Ferragus, bound, unto the city, and having by his spells caused all the Saracen army to sleep soundly, the garrison sallied forth, and slew them to a man. Ferragus was offered his life on condition of his turning Christian; but this he refused, and was beheaded. The Duke of Aquitaine and Orson now resolved to go to the relief of Constantinople, and, aided by a sortie of the garrison, the Saracen army was totally destroyed. The Emperor, King Pepin, Valentine and the Green Knight, then went to meet Bellisant, who had arrived in a ship. She, of course, was reconciled to her husband, and there was universal joy.

Except with Valentine, who missed the face of his beloved Clerimond. On closely questioning Pacolet, he told him how she had been carried off by King Trompart, and he vowed to spend his life in searching for her. From this point the Romance becomes so involved and intricate, as to be somewhat difficult to follow, and I shall simplify it by leaving out a vast amount of extraneous matter, and only follow the fortunes of the principal characters. Valentine and Pacolet travelled in many lands in searching after Clerimond, and met with numberless adventures, until, at last, they met King Pepin, who had been taken prisoner at Jerusalem, and had been interned at the court of the King of India, where he reported Clerimond to be, still faithful to her absent love, having counterfeited madness to avoid the king's love.

Valentine clothed himself in pilgrim's garb, and at once set out for the court of the King of India. Arrived there he gave himself out to be a physician, and a specialist in cases of madness. This caused him to be brought into Lady Clerimond's presence. He discovered himself, and, finding that she had carefully kept Pacolet's horse, they mounted thereon, and safely escaped.

His next exploit was delivering his father, the Green Knight, and the twelve Peers of France, from the hands of the Lady Galazy; and he, in his turn, was afterwards besieged in the city of Angory. His father with ten thousand men came to their relief, and, in order to secure a safe landing, the Emperor ordered that what we should term his staff should put on pagan garments. Valentine saw this band of paynims, charged them, and inadvertently killed his father. There was but scant time for mourning, for the heathen were prevailing, so he and Orson once more joined the fray, and, by their deeds of valour, changed the fortune of war, and completely routed the Saracens. But, after the excitement of battle, came a reaction, and Valentine was as one mad. So, being incapable of attending to affairs, they crowned the Green Knight King of Angory, and departed for Constantinople.

In the meantime things were not going well at the French Court, where Haufray and Henry were. These two, having no Valentine to hate, turned their attention to the young Charlemagne their brother, whom Pepin had made his heir; and, having invited him, and the king and queen, to a feast, they determined to poison him. But he came not, so they gave the poisoned cup to the king and queen, and they both drank, and died. The two wicked brothers seized on all the strong castles and cities, but could not find Charlemagne, who was with his sister; by whose aid, and that of the King of England, Haufray and Henry

were eventually overcome, and slain, whilst Charlemagne
was crowned king, amidst universal joy.

Valentine and Orson went to Constantinople, bearers of
the sad news of the Emperor's death, and, the throne being
vacant, they were chosen joint emperors. But Valentine
governed not long—he was too oppressed by the weight of
the crime he had committed, in unwittingly killing his
father, and he sought the common refuge of the time, a
pilgrimage. He told Clerimond of his resolve, and they
broke her wedding-ring, each keeping half. Then, taking
only one page with him, he set out for Rome, where,
" comming into the presence of a hermit, he confessed the
death of his father ; the hermit seeing him so penitent,
enjoyned him pennance : First change thy habit and go
barely cloathed, and 7 yeares lye under the staires of thy
pallace, without speaking any words ; thou shalt neither
eat nor drinke but of the scraps that come from thine own
table—do thus, and feare not thy sins. Sir, said Valentine,
all this I will do ; so, after he had dined, he departed without speaking to his servant : after this Valentine entred
into a wood, feeding upon Roots ; and he continued there
so long that he was forgotten amongst men."

Valentine followed out the instructions of the hermit,
and lay under the stairs of his own house, none knowing
who the poor pilgrim was. " At the end of seaven yeares
Valentine fell into a mortall disease, whereof he dyed.
Before his death an Angell appeared to him saying, Valen-

tine, thy glasse is run, for within foure houres thou shalt die; whereat he greatly rejoyced, making signes for pen, inke and paper: when he had it, he wrote that it was himselfe that appeared like a Pilgrim. After putting to his name, he closed up the paper, putting in the other halfe of the Ring that he had kept: shortly after he layd him down, and dyed." Clerimond was disconsolate at his death, and ever afterwards lived a single life.

Orson reigned seven years, when he, too, retired into a wood, and lived on roots; and, when he died, he was succeeded in the government by his children. The chronicle finishes thus: "The Green Knight after so governed his children that they carefully spent their time on earth, and followed their Father to his grave."

¶ Syr Eglamoure of Artoys,

Sir Eglamoure of Artoys.

THE British Museum possesses a MS. of this Romance (paper 15th century), and Copland printed a version, which is in the Bodleian Library, but I have taken my story from one in the British Museum printed by John Walley, A.D. 1570.

In the court of Sir Prynsamoure, Earl of Artois, there were many knights, but pre-eminent amongst them, both for courtesy and feats of arms, was Sir Eglamoure. The Earl had but one child, a daughter named Christabel, and she would be his heiress. She was of surpassing beauty, her fair complexion even coming up to the Romance standard—"as whyte as whales-bone." She loved Eglamoure, and he loved her ; and when lords and knights came from strange lands to joust in honour of Christabel, and thus endeavour to win her love, the lance of Sir Eglamoure ever overthrew them. He, although he loved her dearly, had but little hope of winning her, for, besides the presumption of his aspiring to the hand of his patron's daughter, with the chance of succeeding to his sovereignty, he was poor, and, as his chamberlain told him, " a knyght of lytel lande," supplementing this information with the proverb—

> The man that heweth over hye,
> Some chyp falleth in his eye.

This trusty servant endeavoured to prove to his master the hopelessness of his love, pointing out that she was sought for by princes and lords, and that it was scarcely likely she would look favourably on a simple knight. Sir Eglamoure, somewhat discouraged by this conversation, retired to his chamber, where he prayed to God to help him in this strait, and to grant that he might have the Earl's daughter to wife. Then he took to his bed, sick with love.

> On the morowe that mayden small
> Ete wyth her father in the hall
> That was so fayre and bryght.
> All the knyghtes were at mate save he ;
> The ladye sayd for Goddes pytie
> Where is Syr Eglamoure my knyght?
> Hys squyere answered wyth hevy chere,
> He is syke and dead full nere ;
> He prayeth of you a syght.

The Earl told his daughter to go and see the sick knight, for that he was always courteous and kind, besides being first in the tournament. So, after dinner, accompanied by her two maidens, she went to the knight's chamber, and inquired after his health.

> And than sayde that lady bryght,
> How fareth Syr Eglamoure my knyght,
> That is man ryght fayre?
> For sothe lady, as ye may se,
> With wo I am bound for the love of the,
> In longynge and in care.
> Syr, she sayde, by Goddes pytie,
> If ye be agreved for me
> It wolde greve me full sore.
> Damosell, might I tourne to lyfe,
> I wolde have you to be my wyfe
> If it your wyll were.

She replied that she was fond of him, and, if he would speak plainly to her father on the subject, and obtain his consent, she would be willing. The knight was so overjoyed at this *quasi* consent, that he ordered his squire to "fetch an .₵. pounde or two," which he presented to his inamorata's two maids, against their marriage. This generosity was so pleasing to the lady, that she rewarded her love with a kiss. On her return to the palace the Earl inquired after Sir Eglamoure, and she informed him that he was much better, and intended to go out hawking on the morrow; and the Earl was so pleased thereat, that he said he would accompany him.

They rode hawking all next day, and at night, on their return home, Sir Eglamoure spoke to the Earl on the subject of his love for his daughter. His proposition was distasteful to the Earl, but he diplomatically agreed to it,

provided the knight was successful in three deeds of arms,
which he would set him—the first being that he should go
hunting in a forest belonging to a giant named Sir Marocke,
and bring thence a hart.

> The knyght thought on Crystabell,
> He swore by him that harowed hell
> Him wolde he never forsake.
> Syr, kepe wel my lady and my lande,
> Therto the erle helde up his hande,
> And trothes [1] they dyd stryke.

He then went to bid his love farewell, telling her the
errand on which he was bent ; and she gave him a greyhound, from which no deer had ever escaped, and a
sword, which had been found in the sea—

> There is no helme of yron and stele
> But it wolde carve in two.

So he set off on his journey, and soon came to the
giant's forest, where he found abundance of deer ; but
started one hart in particular—the finest of the herd.
The deep baying of the deer-hound woke the giant
Marocke, who had an unconquerable aversion to having
his deer hunted, and he at once roused himself, and went
in search of the poacher. By this time Sir Eglamoure had
killed his deer, and blown a *mort* on his horn, a proceeding
not likely to appease the giant's anger ; so that when they
met but scant courtesy passed, and Marocke smote a
swinging blow with his club, which missed the knight, and

[1] They plighted or pledged their faith.

spent its force on the ground. And then began a mighty combat, which lasted three days, which is the more marvel when we consider that, at the first onset, the glitter of Sir Eglamoure's sword blinded poor Marocke, so that it was much to his credit that the fight lasted so long. At length Marocke was vanquished, and, having cut off his head, Eglamoure took that and the venison to the Earl, in witness that he had accomplished his first task.

He was immediately set another, which was to go to the land of Satyn, wherever that was, and slay a boar which had tusks a yard long, and had so ravaged the country that no man could live there ; indeed, he found his way to the animal by the corpses and skeletons of the men it had slain. Early next day he met this awful beast coming from the sea, where it had been taking its *morning draught*, and when it saw the knight, it began sharpening its tusks as if it were mad. Sir Eglamoure tried the effects of a spear upon it, but it had no effect on its tough hide ; and his horse having been slain by the boar, he had no option but to continue the fight on foot. Again was the combat continued for three days, before the knight was victorious, and could add the boar's head and tusks to his other trophies.

But this time fate ordained that he should not return home at once, for the roars and yells of the boar had attracted the attention of the King of Satyn, who, with his retinue, was out hunting. He thought it was some

man in distress, and sent a squire to see, who arrived just
in time to witness the end of the fight. He reported to
the king, how that a knight had slain the dreaded boar,
and his majesty must needs go and see that doughty
knight. They had their midday meal together under the
shadow of the trees, and the king invited the knight to
spend the night with him, and was especially delighted
when he found that he had slain Marocke, for he was
much troubled with that giant's brother, one Manas.
The invitation was accepted, and, to reinvigorate him
after his recent severe toil—

> Agaynst even the kynge dyd dight
> A bath for that gentle knyght
> That was of herbes good.
> Syr Eglamoure therein laye
> Tyll it was lyght of the daye
> That men to matyns yode.

After he had heard mass, came the giant Manas calling
out to the king, that unless he sent his daughter Ardanata
to him, he would have his blood. Sir Eglamoure could
not brook this insult to his host, so, arming himself, he went
on the walls, commanding a squire to show the giant the
head of the slaughtered boar. At the sight of it Manas
bewailed the loss of his " lytell speckled hoglyne," and
threatened destruction to all concerned in its death. Sir
Eglamoure mounted his steed, couched his spear, and rode
at the giant ; but he might as well have ridden against a
rock—man and horse were overthrown, the latter killed,

the former sore bruised. Sir Eglamoure carried on the combat on foot, cut off the giant's hand, and allowed the huge monster to tire himself out, so that about eventide he killed him. Great was the joye at Satyn, and the king wished to abdicate, and give him not only his kingdom, but his daughter. Sir Eglamoure gratefully declined both, saying he had other work on hand; but the fair Ardanata gave him a ring, which would bear him harmless either on land or water.

Taking the heads both of the giant and the boar, Sir Eglamoure returned to the court of Artois, where his first visit was to his lady love, who sprang to meet him. Having kissed her, he went to the hall to see Earl Prynsamoure, who never expected that the knight could have come safely out of the ordeal; and his disappointment was so great, that he cast aside his previous dissimulation.

> The erle answered, and was full of wo,
> What devyll! may nothynge the slo?
> Forsothe ryght as I wene
> Thou art aboute, as I understande,
> For to wynne Artoys and all my lande,
> And also my doughter clene.

Sir Eglamoure replied that was so, provided he proved himself worthy; and the Earl, thinking that he might fail in the third adventure, wished him to commence it at once. But the knight pleaded the labours and fatigues he had but just undergone, and asked for three months' repose, which was granted.

Syr Eglamoure, after souper,
Went to Crystabelles chamber
With torches brennynge bryght.
The lady was of so great pryde
She set hym on her bedde syde,
And sayde welcome Syr Knyght.
Then Eglamoure dyd her tell
Of adventures that him befell,
But there he dwelled all nyght.
Damosell, he sayd, so God me spede,
I hope to God you for to wedde ;
And then theyr trouthes plyght.

To their mutual grief the three months expired, and the
Earl set Sir Eglamoure his third and final task. He told
him that at Rome there was a dragon, which was of such
might, that it prevented any one from going within five
miles of the city, and his task was to slay the venomous
beast. He set out on his adventure in good spirits, having
taken an affectionate farewell of his lady love, to whom he
gave the gold ring with which Ardanata had presented
him, to keep him in special remembrance.

Arrived at Rome, he soon found the dragon, and in a
short time they were hotly engaged ; but when the dragon
had lost its tail, its head, and its wings, a blow which
cleaved its backbone settled it, and it gave up the ghost.
But this was not achieved without grievous hurt to the
knight. Great rejoicings were at Rome at the slaying of
the dragon, and Constantine, the emperor, gave orders to
fetch the knight with triumph into the city. But Sir
Eglamoure was nearly dead, and it was only the medical

skill of the emperor's daughter, Vyatdurs, that saved his life.

But his healing and convalescence took so long a time, that, ere he could get back to Artois, to claim his guerdon, and wed Christabel, she had borne a son; at which the king was so incensed, that he put her and her little child alone on board a ship, and left them to the mercy of the waves, disregarding all entreaties to the contrary.

In spite of the talismanic ring, the ship, after many days' voyaging, ran on a rock, and left them on a land overrun with wild beasts. With trembling limbs she staggered inland, in great fear, her babe, who was wrapped in a scarlet mantle and gold girdle, in her arms; when a griffin, descending from the skies, snatched at her child, and, tearing it from her, flew away. Words cannot depict her grief. The griffin pursued its way until it came to the kingdom of Israel; and the king of that country, being out hunting, espied the griffin, and made it drop its burden. He took up the boy, carried him home, and, finding from his clothes that he was of gentle blood, brought him up and educated him as his son, christening him Degrabell.

Christabel returned to the ship, which was blown off the rocks, and for five days she drifted about without food, until she arrived on the coast of Egypt. Sir Marmaduke the king, being in his tower, saw the derelict, and sent a squire to inspect it, who reported that it contained but a beautiful female, who could but make signs to him. She was taken on shore, fed well, and then brought before the king, to whom she told her sad tale.   He turned out to be her uncle, and at his court she abode.

The Romance now turns to Eglamoure, who, being whole and sound, was desirous of returning to Artois ; which he did, taking with him the dragon's head.   On his landing, he heard the sad fate of Christabel and their babe.   After fainting, he went in a very excited state to the Earl's hall, where, finding that nobleman, he roughly addressed him—

> And thou erle of Artoys,
> Take, he sayde, the Dragons hede ;
> All is myne that here is leved,
> What doest thou in my place ?

He then called wildly on Christabel, and behaved in such a frenzied way that it is no wonder

> The erle was so ferde of Eglamoure,
> That he was fayne to take the toure.

When he got calmer, he dubbed two and thirty knights, and then he left for the Holy Land, where he abode fifteen years, doing great deeds of arms, both in battle and tournament.

The King of Israel was getting old, and Degrabell, having arrived at a proper age, was by him dubbed knight, and received as arms a golden griffin on an azure field, having in its claws a man child in a mantle, bound with a girdle of gold.   And the old king told him that it was

time he should think about marrying, and that in Egypt
was " a swete thynge."

Although Degrabell was but fifteen years old, he was
taller than the other knights by a foot, and, being considered
perfectly marriageable, the King of Israel set out for Egypt
with Degrabell and a company of knights. On their
arrival,

> The Kynge of Israel on lande goeth,
> The King of Egypt by the hand hym taketh,
> And ledde hym into the hall.
> Syr, sayd the Kynge, for charyte
> Wyll ye let me your daughter se,
> Whyte as bone of whall.
> The lady fro the chambre was brought,
> With mannes hande she semed wrought
> And carved out of tre.[1]
> Her owne sonne stode and behelde,
> Well worthe him that might welde,[2]
> Thus to hymselfe thought he.
> The Kynge of Israel asked than
> If that she myght passe the streme
> His sonnes wyfe for to be.
> Syr, said the Kynge, yf that ye maye
> Mete me a stroke to morrowe daye,
> Thine askinge graunt I the.

On the morrow the lists were prepared, and Degrabell
and King Marmaduke met in mimic combat; but the
former, at the first course, unhorsed the king, a feat which
caused that monarch to say that he was worthy of
Christabel, and the couple were taken to church and
married. But when Christabel saw his arms, she wept full

---

[1] Wood. [2] Govern.

sore, and when questioned on the subject, she told her tale
of how her child had been reft from her by a griffin ; and
the King of Israel joined in with his story of how such a
child had been found.   An *éclaircissement* took place :
the queen recognized in Degrabell her son, he, in her, his
mother, and of course, under these circumstances, the
marriage was considered null.

But her uncle, considering that she ought to be married,
asked her which of the knights she would choose.   In this
matter, however, Degrabell had a word to say, and he
would not consent to his mother marrying any one, except
that he won her in fair fight as he had done ; and as every
lord wished to compete for so fair a prize, it was decided,
and proclaimed far and near, that a tournament should be
held, at an appointed time, to settle their claims.

Sir Eglamoure having by this time tired of living in
Syria, was on his way home, when he heard of this tournament, and determined to be present.   He went there, and
was conspicuous by his beautiful armour, and his heraldic
bearings.

> He beareth in Azure a shyppe of golde,
> Full rychely portreyed in the molde,
> Full well and worthely.
> The see was made both grymme and bolde,
> A yonge chylde of a nyght olde
> And a woman lyenge thereby.
> Of sylver was the mast, of gold the fain,[1]
> Sayle, rope, cabels, echone[2]
> Paynted were worthely.

[1] The weathercock a-top of the mast.   [2] Each or every one.

Degrabell did wonders ; knight succeeded knight only to be worsted, until, last of all, it came to the turn of Sir Eglamoure, who, after a brief parley, engaged with his son. The latter could not stand against the veteran, fresh from his deeds of arms in heathenesse.

> Syr Eglamoure, as it was happe,
> He gave his sonne suche a rappe
> That to the grounde wente he.
> Alas, than sayd lady fare,
> My sonne is dead, by goddes pitie,
> The kene knyght hath hym slayne.

He was only shaken, but the tournament was at an end ; and, after disarming, the knights joined in feasting. Sir Eglamoure, as being the victor, was placed at Christabel's side, and she asked him why he bore such arms. He replied that his lady and his young son had been sent to sea in an open boat by her father. Breathlessly she asked his name, and, when she heard it, she naturally fainted. Mutual explanations took place, and universal joy reigned around. The wedding was settled to take place at Artois, and Sir Eglamoure invited the three kings of Israel, Egypt, and Satyn, to be present—the latter having promised that his daughter Ardanata should marry Degrabell.

Over the sea they went right joyously, and soon arrived at Artois, where

> The erle than in a toure stode,
> He sawe men passe the salt floode
> And fast his horse gan dryve.

Whan he herde of Eglamoure
He fell out of his toure,
And brake his necke belyve.[1]

This event did not in any manner hinder the marriages, which duly took place, graced by the presence of the Emperor Constantine. The King of Israel gave half his land to Degrabell, with the promise of the reversion of the whole at his decease, and

With mykell myrthe the feast was made,
Fourty dayes it abode
Among all lordes hende.[2]
And than forsothe, as I you saye,
Every man toke his owne waye
Where hym lyked to dwell.

[1] Quickly.   [2] Gentle, polite.

Guy of Warwick.

THE British Museum is very rich in MSS. of this Romance — beginning with one of the rarest quality (Harley 3775), vellum, circa 1300. The Royal, Sloane, Additional, Cotton, Harleian, and Lansdowne Collections, all have MSS. of fourteenth and fifteenth century, but the earliest known printed copy is French. " Cy Commence Guy de Warwick, chevalier d'Angleterre, qui en son temps fit plusieurs prouesses et conquestes en Angleterre, en Allemaigne, Ytalie et Dannemarche, et aussi sur les infidelles ennemys de la chrestienete. Par. Fr. Regnault, 7 Mars. 1525." And Hazlitt says that in the Bodleian Library is one leaf containing thirty lines on a page, printed with Wynkyn de Worde's types. I have taken mine from a copy printed by Copland, attributed to 1560 (?).

The fire at Warwick Castle on Advent Sunday, 1871, spared the so-called relics of Guy, and they are now removed from the porter's lodge, . . . where they were formerly kept, to the Great Hall. One William Hoggeson, yeoman of the buttery, had, temp. Henry VIII., 2d. per diem allowed him for the custody of Guy's sword. There are his shield, helmet, breastplate, walking-staff and tilting-pole, all of great size, though the Romance does not speak of his being taller than his fellows—any more than it mentions his slaying a dun cow, which is an article of firm belief in Warwickshire. His porridge-pot is but a garrison crock of the sixteenth century, and his flesh-fork is a military fork, temp. Henry VIII., so that the other relics are probably as authentic.

Earl Rohaunt was not only Earl of Warwick, but of Oxford and Buckingham, and his daughter Phelys, or Phyllis, was not only very beautiful, but as learned as if she had studied at Girton. His estate was well administered by his steward, Segurd of Wallingford, whose son Guy— the hero of the Romance—was of beautiful form and features, graceful, active, and courageous. He was chief cupbearer to the Earl, and in that capacity had ample opportunities of beholding the fair Phyllis, with whom he fell deeply in love.

It was the feast of Pentecost, which was celebrated by the Earl with great solemnity, with jousting, hunting, and hawking, and it so happened that Guy was commanded by his noble master to look after the welfare of the ladies at dinner. His graceful form called forth many a glance from the fair damsels ; and even the incomparable Phyllis, when he presented her with water to wash her hands, as was the custom then, both before and after meat, deigned to ask his name.

From that time Guy's fate was sealed, and he took the bold step of declaring his passion. Phyllis simply treated the youth as an inferior who had been guilty of a grave presumption, and he went away disconsolate. In those days despairing lovers lost flesh rapidly, and were soon brought to death's door, Guy being no exception, and, in spite of the most learned physicians, he was near dying ; and yet these leeches could not diagnose his case, nor say what was his malady, the symptoms, according to an old MS., being—

> In my hed comyth a colde blode,
> That makyth me to qwake, as y were wode ;[1]
> Aftur, comyth a strong hete
> That makyth my body for to swete :
> All I brenne,[2] boone[3] and hyde[4]
> All hote, as any glede.[5]
> Thys ys my lyfe nyght and daye,
> For payne reste y ne maye.

Luckily for him, at this juncture the lady Phyllis had a dream, or, to use a stronger term, angelic vision, in which an angel visited her and bade her love her humble suitor ; and that same night, Guy, feeling his strength almost exhausted, went painfully into the garden, with the

[1] As if I were mad.   [2] Burn.   [3] Bone.   [4] Skin.   [5] A red-hot coal.

determination of making a final appeal to the object of his affection. He found her, with but one attendant, and having told her how he was dying for love of her, he cast himself on the ground swooning. At this her womanly nature asserted itself, and, after he came to himself, she mildly rated him, winding up by telling him that before she could become his wife he must be dubbed a knight.

This set him off swooning again, this time for joy, and when he recovered he went to the Earl, and begged him to knight him. To this Earl Rohaunt consented, more especially as he had a batch of twenty squires on hand, waiting to be dubbed. As soon as he had received his new dignity, he sought Phyllis and pressed his suit, but she gave him to understand that she meant that he must be an approved knight before she would wed him.

> Therefore, Sir Guy, with wordes few,
> My wyll to thee now will I shew :
> At thy wyll gettest thou not mee,
> Tyll thou so doughty a knyght bee,
> That thou have in this worlde no pere,
> In no lande farre ne nere,
> And that thou bere the maystry,
> And floure of all chevalry ;
> And when thou [art] so noble tolde
> That in this worlde be none so bolde,
> Thou shalt then have the love of mee,
> At thy wyll so wyll I be.

Being, probably, well aware of the firm character of his beloved, Guy accepted the situation without murmur; and after kissing her, he went straight to the Earl, and asked

his permission to leave his service, and go across the sea to
seek adventures. Earl Rohaunt asked him why he wanted
to leave, whether he lacked anything ; but, finally, gave his
consent, and Guy went to his parents to acquaint them
with his determination. Both his father and mother tried
to persuade him not to go, but he would not yield ; and,
having received their blessing, he soon set sail.

He landed at Normandy, went to Spain and Germany,
in all of which countries he distinguished himself ; after
which he went to Lombardy, in company with three
knights, Sirs Heraude, Urry, and Thorold. Here Duke
Otho of Pauy (or Pavia), who had been wounded by Guy
in Brittany, instructed fifteen of his knights to waylay our
hero, slay his companions, and bring him to the duke.
But they reckoned not on the prowess of Guy and his
companions ; a fearful fight ensued.   Of Guy's three
knights two were slain, and himself wounded ; yet but
one of the Lombards returned to tell the tale of their
discomfiture to Duke Otho. Heraude was thought to be
dead, but a monk discovered a spark of life in him, and
he eventually recovered.   Guy was healed of his wound,
and afterwards went into Poland, thence to Saxony,
and in both places he was made welcome on account of
his marvellous feats of arms.   Thence he proceeded to
Burgundy, at which court he abode some time.

Here, one day, being hunting, he met with a palmer,
who turned out to be no other than his old knight com-

panion Heraude, who, since his convalescence, had been
seeking Guy. Joyfully they returned together to the
court of the Duke of Burgundy, and, soon after, they took
their leave, with the intention of returning to their own
country. But at Saint Omers they met a palmer who
told them that the Emperor Raynere had besieged Duke
Segwyn of Lavayne, because the latter had slain his
cousin Sadock. If there was any fighting to be done,
Guy must be in it, and, on hearing this news, he and
Heraude made up their minds to go and help the duke ;
and they did so, taking with them fifty knights.

They arrived at Duke Segwyn's town, abode there
all night, and, on the morrow, hearing that the emperor's
troops were advancing, led by his steward, who was a
mighty man of valour, they sallied out, and, aided by a
sortie from the town, utterly routed the Germans, taking
the steward, and several of the nobility, prisoners.

The emperor did not take this reverse kindly, but
threatened to annihilate the duke and Sir Guy ; and Otho
(Guy's old foe) assured the monarch that he should be
well avenged before seven days should have passed.
With him went Raynere, Duke of Saxony, and Wando-
mere, the Constable of Cologne ; but they only went to
defeat, for the troops were routed. Guy sorely wounded
his enemy, Duke Otho, and the other two leaders were taken
prisoners. It was in this battle that Sir Terry, who was
afterwards one of Guy's firmest friends, distinguished
himself mightily.

The emperor was playing at chess, when he saw Sir Terry spurring furiously, drawn sword in hand; all wounded was he, and his armour rent, his hauberk and basinet hacked and hewed. Soon were told his heavy tidings respecting the defeat of the imperial army, and the emperor nearly lost his reason on hearing the bad news; but

> He sware by God, that had him bought,
> He should never be glad in thought
> Till he the Duke had in hande
> And brent and destroyed all his Lande.

So the emperor set out at the head of his army, and with him rode his son Sir Gayre. But when they were come before the town, Guy sallied forth with a thousand knights, and not only took Sir Gayre prisoner, but so demoralized the enemy, that the emperor had to send a reinforcement of two thousand men, who, being more than the besieged cared to cope with, they retired into the shelter of their town, absolutely weary of fighting.

> When the Emperour heard sayne
> That his sonne was taken certayn,
> He sayd, and made an hydyous crye,
> Assayle the Cittie hastily.
> His men so did without fayle,
> The Cittie they faste assayle ;
> Stones they thrue at the towne
> For to fell the walles downe ;
> They shoten with noble albasters [1]
> And great plenty of good Archers ;

[1] Cross-bowmen.

> They clymed upon the walles of stone
> For to take the towne anone ;
> But they within had no doubt,
> With strength ynough they put them out.

And the siege went on, to the great daily loss of the Germans ; till, one day, a spy brought news that the emperor was going to hunt in the forest.   The duke thought to take a great force, with some of his trustiest knights, and capture him, but Guy said that he would undertake the task.   So, taking with him a thousand knights, he rode into the forest, where he found the king hunting.

> With that came Guy forth anone right,
> On a noble steede full fast prickand,[1]
> A branch of Olyve in his hand,
> That betokeneth peace to be ;
> The Emperour well fayre greeted he.
> Guy sayd, God that is full of might,
> Save thee, syr gentle knight,
> And give thy menne happe [2] and grace,
> Well to rede [3] thee in this place.
> Duke Segwyn sendeth me to thee,
> That in good maner will love thee,
> With glad cheare he prayeth you
> To harborow [4] with him now.
> He shall you welcome, and your Barrons,
> With Swannes, Craynes, and Herons,
> And make you right well at ease ;
> These wordes, quod Guy, be no lese.[5]
> Duke Segwyne will yeelde thee
> His Castle and his good Cittie,
> And all landes lowde and still,
> And himselfe at your owne will.

[1] Spurring.   [2] Luck.   [3] Counsel, advice.   [4] Live.   [5] Are true.

Therfore, Syr, I warne you
To him ye must with me now,
For what more can he to thee do,
Than thus meekely send thee to?

But although Guy said that he was speaking without
" lese," both the parties knew that it meant capture and
polite imprisonment. The emperor, for form's sake, consulted with the King of Hungary, Duke Otho, Sir Terry,
and others of his nobility, and decided to endorse the
fiction, and go to visit Duke Segwyn as his guest.

Arrived at the city, Sir Guy did the honours, Segwyn
keeping out of sight ; as indeed he did until he had seen
the knights and barons his prisoners, whom he begged to
intercede for him with the emperor. This they willingly
agreed to do; and the duke appeared before his imperial
master barefoot and in his shirt only, with an olive branch
in his hand, and, falling on his knees, he begged forgiveness—

And said, Syr, mercy certayne
I will no more warre thee agayne,
For that I have grevyd thee yll,
I and all myne is at thy wyll.

He pleaded that Sadock had but himself to thank for
his death, having provoked the quarrel which led to their
combat ; but, if the king thought fit, he would sustain
his cause to be righteous, with his body. The emperor's
nobility interceded in his behalf, led by the imperial heir,
Sir Gayre, who spoke thus :

> Father, he sayd, by Saynt Martyn
> A noble man is Duke Segwyn,
> And a doughty man of dede ;
> He may you helpe at your neede.
> Forgyve him, I pray you now,
> That he hath trespassed agaynst you ;
> Or, certes, syr, sayd he,
> Love get ye none of me.

Guy added his intercession, and the emperor forgave the duke freely ; an act which did not pass without comment among his peers—one of whom, Duke Otho, stigmatized the emperor as a " false traytour " for making friends with one who had shed a kinsman's blood. The fiery Guy at once wanted to fight him ; peace was with difficulty restored, and a double marriage cemented this reconciliation.

> Then wedded Duke Raynere, with glee,
> Segwyn's syster, a mayden free,
> And led her, as I understand,
> To Burntswick his owne lande.
> Then sayde the riche Emperour
> To Duke Segwyne, wyth great honour,
> Now never more to be at stryfe,
> Therefore I will give thee a wyfe,
> A fayre mayden that is niece myne.
> Gramercy, Syr, sayd Duke Segwyne.
> Of them was made a fayre wedding.

After the usual festivity, Sir Guy took his leave, and accompanied the emperor ; and, as they went on their way, occasionally hunting and hawking, he espied a dormound,[1] and immediately interrogated the skipper, as

[1] A dromond, or armed vessel.

to what country he was of, &c. " Sayd a marryner full
tight " that they hailed from Constantinople, and that a
Soudan, or Sultan, had invaded their territory with sixty
thousand men, and had besieged the Greek emperor,
Ernis, had destroyed all his troops, and taken all his land,
save that city.

On hearing this, Guy consulted with his old friend
Heraude, and the upshot was, that, refusing the " landes
and fee " offered him by the Emperor of Germany, he
chose a thousand knights, and with them immediately set
sail. The distressed Grecian emperor received them with
effusion, and offered his daughter to Guy in marriage.
Sir Guy and his knights turned the tide of war; they
defeated the Soudan's troops, Guy killed his nephew,
Coldran, and so grievously wounded Eskeldart, who was
the Saracen's chief general, that he had but time to reach
home before he died, having told his tale to his master,
the Soudan, who vowed he would destroy Constantinople.

But Guy had foes within doors, as well as without. The
emperor had promised him great rewards, and, among
them, the hand of his daughter, Loret; but the steward of
the Emperor of Germany, one Morgradour, loved her, and
would fain have both her and her father's dominions. This
he essayed to compass by craft, and, pretending a great
love for Guy, he one day suggested that they should go and
have a game at chess in the fair Loret's chamber—which
they accordingly did ; but, on the conclusion of the game,

Morgradour made some excuse and left the room, taking horse, however, immediately, and rushing off to the Emperor Ernis to tell him that Guy was in his daughter's chamber, whither he had gone with felonious intent, and counselled Guy's instant hanging—in which case he promised he would go to the Emperor of Germany, and bring such a force as would completely rid Ernis of his enemies. But the latter could not believe the steward.

> Then sayd Ernis the Emperour,
> Let be thy tales, Morgradour,
> That gentle knight would not doe this
> For all the Empyre, I wys.

So the false traitor rode back to Sir Guy, and told him how the emperor had made such an accusation against him, and was coming to hang him. Guy believed his lying words, and, determining not to stop to be hanged, he gathered his knights together, explained to them the situation, and told them he was going to join the emperor's enemies. But, as they were putting their plan into execution, they met the emperor, and, after a few words of explanation, they were reconciled.

The next day was a great battle with the Saracens, ending in the defeat of the latter; an event which had a peculiar effect upon the Soudan, who attributed it to the inefficacy of his gods.

> Then sayd the Soudan so grim,
> To bring his Gods before him,

Gods, he sayd, evil mote ye be,
For evil, he sayd, have ye quit me.
With honour, he sayd, I have served you,
And will I have my meede [1] now.
Therefore I shall on you bewreke,[2]
All your neckes I shall doe breake.
He began to lay on fast,
While a staffe in his hande might laste,
He all to hew them and gan fayne,
Ye shall be brent, forsooth, certayne ;
For ye be worse than houndes,
That ever I saw ye wo be the stounds.[3]
Some he brent on a low,[4]
And some into the sea gan throw.

In the meantime, the grateful Emperor Ernis was loading
Sir Guy with favours.

That good Emperour Ernis,
Through Guye's helpe to winne him pryce,[5]
Syr Guy he gave a royall bone,[6]
With all his Lande his will[7] to done.

But this only excited the envy and hatred of Sir
Morgradour, who, knowing that the Soudan would kill
any messenger sent to him, suggested to the emperor
that he should send Sir Guy and Sir Heraude as ambassa-
dors to the paynim sovereign, with the proposition that,
in order to prevent the effusion of any more blood, a
champion should be chosen on either side, by whose fate
both parties should abide, the same as if both armies
engaged and one was victorious. The emperor thought

[1] Reward. [2] Avenge. [3] Moments or time. [4] In a bright fire.
[5] Prize. [6] Boon. [7] To have sole authority over his land.

·the advice good, and caused all his barons to be assembled;
. which was done, and the situation was explained to them :

> But in that hall was none tho
> That durst profer him to go.

Indeed, an old white-bearded knight rose up and denounced
as a traitor whoever had given the emperor such advice,
reminding his sovereign of the fate of his cousin Griffon,
who, being sent with a message to the Sultan, was slain,
and his head returned as answer, adding that it was not
through cowardice that he spoke thus, but through his
advanced age, it being a hundred years since he had been
dubbed knight ; but, had he been in his lusty youth, he
would have undertaken the embassage, well knowing he
was going to his death. This, however, did not fire the
souls of any in that assemblage, save only Guy and
Heraude, the latter chafing, and wishing to spring to his
feet, being only withheld by Guy, who wished to see
whether any would offer.

But no knight was bold enough, so Guy stood up and
accepted the adventure ; but the emperor, who could not
afford to lose him, replied that he had only propounded
the task to try which of his barons and knights would do
the most for him. Guy would not retract his offer, and all
the emperor and his court could do, was to pray for his
success and safe return.

When fully armed, Guy rode forth on his adventure,
and went through the heathen camp, until he saw a

pavilion, on which was an enormous carbuncle ; and, by this, he guessed it was the Soudan's, and there he saw that. sovereign sitting at meat with ten kings, and all his barons round him.   Riding up to them, he opened his embassy in the following extraordinary manner, which would seem but little calculated to achieve the desired object.

> Lorde, that shape, both hote and colde,
> And all this world hath in holde,
> And suffered on Crosse passyons fell
> To buy man's soule out of hell,
> Give the Soudan his malison,[1]
> And all that leeven [2] on Mahouwne ;
> God's curse have thou and thyne,
> And tho that leeve on Apolyne.

He then proceeded to deliver the emperor's message. That he was allowed to do so quietly, speaks volumes for the well-disciplined tempers of the Saracens ; the Soudan, in his astonishment, merely asking

> . . . What art thou
> That thus proudly speakest now?
> Yet found I never man certayne,
> That such wordes durst me sayne.

When Guy declared his name, the Soudan remembered all the evil this terrible warrior had wrought him, and at once decreed his death, commanding him to be kept in prison until dinner was finished.   But our hero did not wait for this command to be obeyed ; he rode straight at the Soudan, cut off his head, and, taking it in his left

---

[1] Curse.   [2] Believe.

hand, he charged through the Saracen host, killing all who
opposed.   Superior numbers, however, told upon him, and
he was sorely pressed, when Heraude, who had been
warned of his friend's need in a dream, came with a strong
body of German knights, turned the tide of battle, and
escorted the victorious Guy to the emperor, to whom he
delivered the Soudan's head.

> And all the belles of the Citie
> Rong with great solemnitie.
> Agayn[1] Syr Guy the people came tho,
> And every man blessed him also,
> And sayd Christ give him good fare,
> That thus hath brought us out of care.

Sir Guy took an original method of disposing of his
enemy's remains, for he had the Soudan's head enclosed in
brass, richly gilt, and set upon a marble pillar in the midst
of the market-place.

In those days people were restless, and the emperor,
having no war on hand, resolved on a tour through his
dominions, to see each town, and repair the ravages of the
Saracens.   Sir Guy, of course, accompanied him, and it
fell on a summer's day that he saw a dragon chasing a
lion.   This was a temptation too great for Guy.

> To his knightes then said Guyon,
> I will go fyght agayne yonder Dragon,
> That would slea yonder gentle Beast;
> Abyde me here, both moste and least.

[1] Opposite, right before.

A terrific combat naturally ensued, which, of course, ended in a victory for Guy, who cut off the dragon's head; nor would the fight travel out of the ordinary canons of romance, were it not for the peculiar behaviour of the lion, who proved himself indeed a " gentle Beast."

> Guy tourned his horse and rode agayne,
> The Lyon him followed, and was full fayne ;
> Before his horse that Lyon ran,
> As comely as any man.
> And for fayne played before Guyon,
> For Guy had slayne that foule Dragon.
> Guyes horse necke the Lyon ran to,
> Guy weened he would have him misdo,
> And downe he sterte [1] full right
> With the Lyon there for to fight.
> And when he was start adowne,
> As still as a Lamb lay the Lyon,
> And there licked he Guyes feete.
> And when Guy saw he was so meeke,
> Guy would him no harme do,
> But let him ren by him tho.
> And everywhere Guy can ride
> The Lyon ran alway by his side.
>
> *   *   *   *   *
>
> At night when Guy yede his chamber to,
> The Lyon him followed him fast tho ;
> On nightes when Guy slept fast perfay, [2]
> The Lyon before his bed lay.

The emperor now thought that it was time for Guy to enter into the fulness of his reward, and made arrangements that he should be married, on the morrow, to his daughter

---

[1] Leaped.   [2] *Par foi*—i' faith.

Loret, with whom, as dowry, he gave half his kingdom ; but when

> The Wedding Ring was forth brought,
> Guy then on fayre Phelis thought,

and fainted. When he came to, he begged that the marriage might be postponed until he had recovered of his illness.; then went home, and took to his bed, where he lay a fortnight, to the great grief of the lion, who would neither eat nor drink. After the fortnight, Guy got up, and went to the emperor, followed by the lion, who accompanied them to dinner, where he lay at his master's feet. He afterwards went to lie down in an arbour, where he was espied by the false Morgradour, who mortally wounded him with his sword. The "gentle Beaste" had just sufficient strength to crawl to his master's chamber and lick his hand, when he expired. Guy was mad, for he would not have lost his pet for "a thousand pound of treasure," and he went to the court, questioning all he met, if they knew who had done this mean deed. No one knew, until he came to a maiden who had seen Sir Morgradour commit the foul act. No sooner did Guy hear this than he sought the villain, and, after a very brief parley, settled accounts with Sir Morgradour, by cleaving his head in two.

Having thus done, Guy sought the emperor, and explained that he must no longer stay with him, for the loss of the German emperor's steward would cause "strained relations" between the sovereigns if he did ; to avoid

which, he proposed to start at once for his own country.
The emperor tried to dissuade him, repeating his offers of
his daughter's hand, and the half of his kingdom ; but

> Syr Emperour, then sayd Guy,
> To wedde yet I am not ready ;
> For if I tooke thy Daughter, certayne
> All thy men would have disdayne
> That thou wouldst make an Emperour
> Of a pore Vavasour.[1]

So if Guy would *not* stay, the emperor was obliged to let
him go. But, if his desire really had been to reach England

quickly, destiny was against him, and he had numerous
adventures before he did so, the principal of which was his
being of much use to, and making a comrade of, Sir Terry,
of whom the Chronicle has before spoken—but, as these
adventures have no real bearing on the story, and are
peculiarly involved and wearisome, I omit them.

> Guy tooke leave, I understande,
> And passed fayre into Englande.

[1] Vassal.

And when Guy was on Englande syde,
Unto Yorke then he gan ryde.
King Athelstone there he founde,
And all the states of the Lande.

Athelstan was delighted to welcome such a Paladin, and was asking after his adventures and welfare, when a messenger came to the king, informing him that there was a foul dragon in Northumberland, who had ravaged twenty miles round it, a fearsome and ugly beast, who slew all who attempted to kill it. Athelstan was at his wit's end how to deal with this evil creature, until Guy solved the difficulty, by proposing that he should go against the dragon, accompanied only by Sir Heraude, and three other knights. Leave was granted him, and they set off at once, soon reaching Northumberland, where no time was lost in finding the habitation of the dragon. On viewing the huge saurian, Guy determined to undertake the adventure by himself, and, having dismissed his comrades, he prayed most heartily for success. The fight was obstinate, for Sir Guy's weapons made no impression on the animal's hard scales, and it was only by ramming his sword down the beast's throat,

That the Dragon began to yell,
As it had bene a fiende of hell ;

and finally gave up the ghost. He then went to Lincoln, where the king then was, and presented him with the dragon's head ; after which he set his face homeward. Arrived at Wallingford, he found both his father and mother dead, and, having given the inheritance he received from them to Sir Heraude, he set his face towards Warwick. Here, like a true lover, he at once sought Phyllis, telling her all his adventures, and how he had refused all women for her sake. She, on her part, declared that she never loved any one as well as she did him; which was all singularly *à propos*, for her father called her to him, told her it was about time she married, and bade her choose some one. She named Sir Guy—a choice which met with Earl Rohaunt's hearty approval, and they were duly married.

But quiet domestic felicity soon palled upon the roving and adventurous Guy, and his married life had lasted but forty days, when,

> After it fell upon a day,
> As Syr Guy came from play,
> Into a toure he went on hye,
> And looked about him farre and nye.
> Guy stoode and bethought him tho
> How he had done many a man wo,
> And slayne many a man with his hande,
> Brent and destroyed many a Lande ;
> And all was for a woman's love,
> And not for God's sake above :

and, pondering over these things, he determined to do penance for his misspent life, in going a pilgrimage to the Holy Land. Not even the tender expostulations of his newly married bride, nor the thought of the child she should bear, made his determination waver for an instant.

The child, when born, he bade her put under the care of his friend Heraude ; and, finding that nothing could turn his will, his wretched wife gave him a gold ring, so that when he looked upon it he might remember her : and he took his departure. The deserted Phyllis, when she fully comprehended the situation, " drue out a little knyfe " wherewith to end her life ; but she thought of her unborn babe, and refrained—taking the more sensible step of consulting her father, who comforted her by suggesting that Guy had only done this to try her, and that he would soon return. Sir Heraude, too, disguised as a palmer, went in quest of him ; but, although he wandered all over Europe, yet he heard no tidings of him, and in due course Phyllis became a mother, and her son was christened Raynburne.

Guy, in his travels, soon met with an adventure, championed the cause of a Sir Tryamoure, whose son Fabour had had the bad luck to checkmate, at chess, the son of the Soudan, who lost his temper, and hit Fabour over the head with the board—a compliment which Fabour returned with interest, killing the Soudan's son with the chess-board. Guy's adversary was, as usual, a giant, but he met at Guy's hands the usual fate of giants, and was killed. He next met his old friend Sir Terry, who was in great tribulation ; but Guy effectually succoured him, and, at length, returned to England.

Things had not gone smoothly at home whilst he was away. His son Raynburne was brought up by Phyllis

until he was four years old, when she, as her husband
wished, handed him over to Sir Heraude for tuition. But
whilst in his care, a great mishap fell upon the child.

> So on a day, I understande,
> Marchauntes came into Englande,
> Into London out of Russye,
> With Englishmen to sell and buy ;
> They gave King Athelstone sylver and golde,
> To buy and sell where they would.
> So on a day, withouten lye,
> The Sarasyns this chylde gan espye,
> Guyes sonne fayre Raynburne,
> And stale him away with treason.

And then they sailed away, until they came unto the land
of a king named Aragus, to whom they made the boy a
present ; and Aragus grew very fond of him, and had the
lad taught all martial exercises ; made him in the course of
years a knight and his chamberlain, gave him fine armour
and good steeds—presents for which he evinced his
gratitude by overthrowing all comers in the tourneys.

Such was the state of Sir Guy's domestic affairs on his
return to England ; and public matters were in a very bad
way, for Havelock King of Denmark, and Conelock King
of Norway, had landed, and burnt every town until they
came to Winchester, where King Athelstan was, and they
were then besieging that city, but they had promised relief,
if Athelstan would find any one to fight their noted but
ill-favoured giant, Colbrond. No champion could be found
in Winchester, but, in answer to prayer, the king had a

vision, that if on the morrow he would go to the gate of
the city, he should find a pilgrim, who would be the
champion.   This the king did.

> And as the Aungell sayd to him,
> At the gate he founde the Pilgrime.
> He led him unto his chamber soone,
> And fell on his knees before him anone ;
> He prayed him that Battayle to doe.
> Redest ¹ thou me to fight, quod Guy, whereto
> Seest thou not me readily,
> Unneathes² for feeblenesse alyve am I.
> Nevertheless, sayd Guy, ryse up, Syr King,
> Syth thou prayest me this thing,
> For thee I shall the battayle do
> If God send me life thereto.
> Well glad was then all Englande,
> That they had agayne Colbronde
> A man lyke for to fight,
> And for to defende their Landes right.

The fight with Colbrond was no child's-play ; heavy
strokes made deep wounds, and the combat seemed likely
to end in the giant's favour, when Guy's sword broke.   In
vain he asked Colbrond to lend him one of his axes—a
courtesy which he did not see his way to grant ; but, by his
superior agility, Guy possessed himself of one, and, with
one sweeping stroke, Colbrond's head was severed from his
body.

The Danes, nearly mad at the loss of their champion,
honourably kept their pact, and retired to their ships ;
and in England was great joy, ringing of .bells, processions

¹ Dost thou counsel me to fight ?   ² Literally *unwieldy*, unfit.

and Te Deums.   But the hero of the day would join in no
merriment, he put on his palmer's weeds and went away,
no man knowing who he was, save only the king, and he

pledged his royal word not to divulge it until his champion
should be dead and buried.   In this humble guise he
reached Warwick, and came to his own gate, where he sat

down among the poor, none recognizing him, making one of the twelve poor men that Phyllis fed every day.

> The Countesse beheld him than,
> For he was so feeble a man.
> Of all her meate she did cheare,
> And to Syr Guy she let it beare,
> And of the best wyne that she had,
> To Guy she sent and bad him be glad.
> And, for she thought him porest of all,
> She bad him eate every day in the hall.

But Guy was satisfied—he had seen his wife, found her full of works of mercy and charity ; but she knew him not, and he turned his steps away from his own home to Arderne, where he found a deserted hermitage, which was to be his home for the short time he had to be on earth. And there he lived in pious contemplation, serving God after his way, and living frugally on the herbs of the field, until one night he had a vision of an angel—

> An Aungell came from God Almighty,
> And said Guy make thee ready ;
> Within this ʋii nights thou shalt come
> To Jesu and in his blisse wone.
> Guy thanked Christ and called mercy,
> So glad was he never erst ¹ truely.

On the seventh day he called his page to him, and bade him go to Warwick, and there call upon the Countess, and show her a gold ring, which he gave the page, and tell her that it came from the pilgrim to whom she sent meat to eat in her own hall—bidding her come with him to Arderne,

¹ Truly was he never so glad before.

a service for which she would well requite him. The page did as he was told, and Phyllis, on seeing the ring, fainted thrice ; after which she could not make haste enough to join her husband, but, under the guidance of the page, she, accompanied by a retinue of knights and squires, rode with all speed to the hermitage, where they found Sir Guy lying on the floor, *in extremis*.

> Then set she up a shrieke so spert,[1]
> For sorow of him nye brast her harte,
> Guy kest[2] up his eyen tho,
> The soule out of the body can go.
> She fell on him in that hermytage,
> She kist his mouth and his vysage,
> Out of his mouth came a savour
> Also sweate as any flower.
> She prayed all the Bishops of the country,
> At her Lordes burying for to be.
> At Warwick he should him grave,
> But no man might[3] him thence have,
> Then bad she let him be.
> In that hermytage buryed was he ;
> A richer burying then she made one,
> King ne Duke had never none ;
> Many a Masse for him was sayde,
> Or he in his grave was layde.

But Phyllis so took Sir Guy's death to heart, that she at once fell ill from grief, and, fifteen days after her husband's decease, she died, leaving instructions that she should be buried by his side, which was accordingly done.

> Now be they both with God Almighty
> Up in hye blisse,
> Jesu us all thereto wish.

[1] Sudden.   [2] Cast up, opened his eyes.   [3] Move.

To complete the story, it now remains but to follow the fortunes of Raynburne, Guy's son ; and to do this, it is necessary to go back to the time of his capture by the Saracens. It will be remembered that he was, at that time, under the tuition of Sir Heraude, who was furious when he discovered the loss of his ward. He did the best thing that could be done under the circumstances : he went at once in pursuit, but was unfortunately wrecked upon the coast of Africa, and, after a fight with the natives, was overpowered and cast into a dungeon, where he lay for many years, until he was overheard lamenting his sad fate, he who had been the boldest baron of his time. This was told the king of that country, who was at that time at war with Aragus, who had protected Raynburne, and, indeed, this latter was at the head of his army, performing prodigies of valour. Feeling the need of every brave arm, he had him taken out of prison, and well bathed and fed, and was overjoyed when he heard that his captive was the redoubt-able Sir Heraude, companion in arms with the invincible Sir Guy : and he offered him his ransom, and a hundred pounds yearly, if he would fight for him against his enemies. To this Sir Heraude consented, and his health and strength were soon recruited by good food.

When he met the Saracens, he slaughtered them in the good old style, and would have slain Aragus, had he not been protected by Raynburne. Of course Heraude had to fight this champion, and this combat was so protracted

and fierce, that each gained a mutual admiration of the
other's prowess ; so that when, during a pause, they learned
each other's names, there was a most affecting meeting
between them, and, by their efforts, a peace was concluded
between the contending parties. They then set their faces
towards England, which they reached after many adventures.

Then passed they, I understande,
The sea and came into Englande ;
To London that they came anone,
And there they found King Athelstone.
Of Heraudes comming glad was he,
And great joy he made them all three.[1]
The King yeelded up Syr Raynburn
His Fathers Landes, tower and towne,
And there were they fower dayes or five,
And after went to Warwick blive.[2]
Men of the countrey, old and yong,
Were glad ynough of their coming ;
Olde and yong, eche man of his age,
Came and did Raynburne homage.

[1] The third was Aslake, a son of Sir Heraude.
[2] Quickly.

Robert the deuyll.

Robert the Devyll.

THIS Romance was early printed in France, for it was published at *Lyons* by P. Mareschall in 1496 ; another edition was issued by Nic. de la Barre, *Paris* 1497 ; and we, too, have very early English versions of the tale, in two editions, but slightly varying, printed by Wynkyn de Worde—one in the Public Library at Cambridge, the other in the British Museum, from which I have taken my story.

The opening sentence of this Romance epitomizes the whole story. " ¶ Here begynneth the lyfe of the moast myschevoust Robert the deyvyll whiche was afterwarde called the servaunt of god." For of all incarnate fiends, he seems to have been one of the worst, and, in his conversion, he shone as a bright example to even professed pietists.

" It befel in tyme past there was a duke in Normandye

whiche was called Ouberte, yᵉ whiche duke was passynge ryche of goodes and also vertuous of lyvynge, and loved and dred god above all thynge and dyde grete almesse dedes, and exceded all other in ryghtwysnesse and justyce, and moost chevalrouse in dedes of armes and notable actes doynge. This duke held open hous upon a crystmasse daye in a towne whiche was called Naverne upon the Seyne. To the whiche courte came all yᵉ lordes and noble blode of Normandy. And bycause this noble duke was not maryed, his lordes, nobles, with one assente besought hym to marye and take a wyfe, to th' entente that his lynage myght be multyplyed thereby, and that they myght have a ryght heyre to enherite his landes after his dyceyse."

In a most complacent manner, he replied that what they said must be right, and that, perhaps, they would kindly " purvey " him a wife. They told him that he spoke " very wysely, and lyke a noble prynce," and one of them said he knew the very lady fitted for the position, the daughter of the Duke of Burgundy. This settled the matter—" This lady was demaunded of her fader, the duke of Bourgone, which gave hym her wyllyngly," and the marriage was celebrated with all the usual ceremonies and festivity.

Years rolled on (the chronicler says eighteen), and to their great grief their union was not blessed with any children—a source of the deepest disappointment to them ; and they were always lamenting the fact, so much so that they came to the conclusion that " they that made the maryage betwene us bothe they dyde grete synne." Still, they did not abandon all hope of offspring, the father praying devoutly for a son and heir who might honour and serve the Lord ; but his wife replied, " In the devyles name be it, insomoche as god hath not y^e power that I conceyve, and yf I be conceyved with chylde, I gyve it to y^e devyll body and soule."

When the child, thus dedicated to the foul fiend, was born, " they were gretly abasshed and aferde with the merveylouse noise and tokens that they herde and se in y^e byrth of the sayd Robert the devyll, in that (when) this chylde was borne, the skye waxed as darke as though it had been nyghte, as it is shewed in olde cronycles that it thondreth and lyghtened so sore that men thought ye firmament had been open and all ye worlde sholde have perysshed. And there blewe soo moche wynde out of the iiij quarters of the worlde, and was suche storme and tempest, that al the hous trembled so sore that it shoke a grete pece of it to ye erth, insomoche that all they that were in ye hous wened that ye worlde had ben at an ende, and that they with ye hous and all sholde have sonken ; but in shorte tyme it pleased God that all this trouble ceased, and the weder clered up, and ye chylde was brought to chyrche to be crystned whiche was named Roberte."

He was so opposed to this Christian rite that he never ceased crying and howling ; and he was obliged to be brought up by hand, and fed with a horn, because he bit his nurse's breasts.   And his growth was also phenomenal, for, at twelve months old, he was as big as a child of three years.   " And the elder that this chyld Robert waxed, more curster ; and there was no man that coud rule hym, and whan he founde or coude come by ony chyldrene he smote and bote [1] and cast stones at them, and brake theyr armes and legges and neckes, and scratte out theyr eyes out of theyr hedes, and therein was all his delyte and pleasure." No wonder, then, that when the street boys saw him " they durst not abyde hym, but cryed one to another here cometh the wode [2] Robert ; and other many cryed here cometh ye cursed madde Robert, and some cryed here cometh Robert ye devyll ; and thus cryenge they voyded [3] all the streets, for they durst not abyde and loke hym in the

---

[1] Beat.   [2] Mad.   [3] Emptied.

face. And forthwith yᵉ chyldrene that knewe hym with one assent called hym Roberte ye devyll, whyche name he kepte durynge his lyfe, and shall do as longe as the worlde standeth."

Vain was the attempt to bring this young demon under scholastic discipline ; for, having found a man bold enough to become his schoolmaster, the pedagogue would fain chastise him for some fault, but Robert " gate a murderer or bodkyn and thrast his mayster in the bely that his guttes fell at his fete, and so fell downe deed to yᵉ erth." From this time none could be found to undertake his education, but all were glad to let him alone and go his own ways, a privilege of which he fully availed himself, becoming a terror to all men, and causing his father many times to wish him dead.

When he was eighteen years old, his mother besought the duke to knight him, so that he might have some employment ; and he consented, telling his son that he did so in order that he might forsake his " vyces and moost hatfull lyf," and live as a chivalrous knight should do. Robert's answer was typical of him. " I shall doo your commaundement, but as for yᵉ ordre of knyghthode, I set nothynge therby, for there is no degre shall cause me (to) leve my condycyons nor change my lyfe ; for I am not in that mynde to do no better than I have done hitherto, nor to amende for no man lyvynge." This gracious reception of an honour was followed by equally bad conduct in church, on the night before he was dubbed, when, according to custom, he watched his armour in church: " theder cam Robert lyke a madman, and overthrowynge al them that came in his waye, ferynge nother god nor ye devyl, and he was never styll of all ye nyght."

This " Mirror of Chivalry," at his first tournament, over-threw all comers, killing and wounding them to such an extent that the king stopped the tourney; which made Robert mad, and he went about smiting those he had killed, till the people rose with one accord and plainly told the duke that he must keep his son under some control. But this hopeful went on his way, committing all kinds of deviltry, murdering, robbing and burning abbeys, churches, hermitages and farms, until there were none left for him to pillage. " These wycked dedes of Robert came to ye eres of ye good duke, and al they that were thus robbed and rebuked, came to complayne of the grete outrage and suppression done by Robert and styll was doynge thorowe-out all the countree. One sayd my lorde youre sone hath forsed my wyfe, an other sayd he hathe ravyshed my doughter, the other sayd he hath stolen my goodes and robbed my hous, and other sayd he hath wounded me to death, with many semblable [1] offences."

His father knew not how to answer these tales of outrage, and sought refuge in prayer—a course which was not immediately efficacious ; till one of his knights spoke up

[1] Similar.

boldly, and told the duke that his advice was that Robert should be sent for, and rebuked before all the nobles, and commanded to alter his style of living ; and, if he would not, then justice should be done upon him as upon a stranger. This advice the duke thought to be good, and acted upon it, sending out men to bring his son to his presence. But Robert evilly entreated his father's messen-

gers, and put out their eyes, mockingly exclaiming, " Syrs, nowe shall ye slepe the better ; go now home to my fader, and tell hym that I set lytel by hym, and bycause he sendeth you to brynge me to hym, therefore to his dyspyte I have put out your eyen."

The poor duke mourned over his maimed servants, but was, as usual, powerless to suggest a remedy ; until one of

his nobles advised his weak-minded lord that it was useless to think that Robert would come, voluntarily, to be
admonished and punished, but, as it was necessary for the
common weal that it should be done, stronger steps should
be taken. Then the duke, willing to follow the counsel of
his nobles, sent in all haste to all ports, cities, and towns,
throughout his dominions, commanding all sheriffs, bailiffs,

and other officers, to use their utmost diligence to bring
his recalcitrant son before him, or to keep him and all his
company safely in prison. When Robert heard of this
proclamation, "he was almoost out of his wyt for wode
angre, and wheted his teeth lyke a bore, and swore a grete
othe, sayenge thus, that he wolde have open warre agenst
his fader, and subdewe and spyll all his lordshyppe."

He evidently thought that his father was in earnest, for he built himself a strong castle in which to defend himself, and there he gathered together "all yᵉ moost myschevouste and falsest theves that he could fynde or here of in his faders lande; to wete morderers, theves, strete robers, rebelles, brenners of chyrches and houses, forsers of women, robbers of churches, and the moost wyckeedest and curseste theves that were under the sonne." With this goodly company he solaced himself with murdering merchants, and plundering all that came in his way, even down to the poor pilgrims, so that every man fled from him, like sheep from a wolf; nay, he even, in one of his mad fits, killed seven holy hermits, "and after that he hadde done this myschevous dede, he rode out of yᵉ wode lyke a devyll out of helle, semynge worse thenne wode, and his clothes were all dyed red with yᵉ blode of the people that he had murdred and slayne, and thus arayed he rode over the felds, and clothes, hands, and face, all were rede of the blode of the holy heremytes, whiche he had so pyteously murdred in the wyldernesse."

In this mad guise he rode recklessly, until he came to the Castle of Darques, where a shepherd had told him his mother was going to dine, and when he came there all men ran from him, shutting themselves in their houses; and, seeing himself thus universally shunned, he fell a-thinking as to why he was leading such a mischievous and cursed life. In this unwonted frame of mind he lighted from off his horse, and, drawing his bloody sword, he strode into the hall where his mother was. She was sore afraid, and would have fled from him, but he called out to her to stay, for pity's sake, until he had spoken to her ; and then he questioned her whether she knew of any reason, or could account for the fact, that he was so vicious, for he was convinced that he had inherited his disposition either from her or his father.

When the duchess heard him speak thus, she fell to, weeping bitterly, and entreated her son to cut her head off. But even Robert's ill-regulated mind recoiled from such a deed, and he asked : " O ! dere moder, why sholde I do so that so moche myschefe have done, and this sholde be the worste dede that ever I dyde." Then the duchess told her son how she had given him over to the devil, adding, " O ! sonne, I am the moost unfortunate woman lyvynge, and I knowlege that it is all my faute that ye be soo cursed and wycked a liver." On hearing this sad tale Robert fainted away, and, on his recovery, fell a-weeping, vowing that henceforth he would do no more harm, but only good, and would amend his life, and do penance for his past sins.

Then, taking leave of his mother, he sought his companions, whom he rebuked for their vicious lives, and exhorted them to change their way of life and repent, adding that he himself was going on a pilgrimage to Rome. His band did not believe in this sudden conversion of their leader, and mocked him, saying, " Now Syrs, take hede ; yᵉ fox wyll be an aunker,[1] for he begynneth to preche." Once more Robert urged them to repentance, but they told him that in future they meant to do more wickedness than in the past. Finding that his exhortations produced no good effect on the reprobate crew, he adopted a highly original method of preventing their doing any mischief ; he killed them all, one after the other, and, locking up his castle, he sent the key to his father, who restored, as far as possible, to the poor people the goods of which his son had robbed them.

In great pain, and poverty, Robert performed his pilgrimage to Rome, where he found the Pope officiating in St. Peter's Cathedral. Could he but reach the Holy Father, and pour his tale of sin into his ears, then, thought he, there might be hope even for him ; so he pressed hard to get to the Pope, but was smitten and told to go back. However, the more he was rebuffed, the more pertinacious he was in his resolve, and made such a noise, that he attracted the attention of the Pontiff, who had pity on him, and desired the people to let him alone. The Pope asked him his business, and Robert told him he was the greatest sinner in the world, and begged the Pope to hear his confession and grant him absolution. The Holy Father asked his name, and when he heard that his penitent was no other than the redoubtable Robert the Devil, he said he would hear his confession, on condition that he would

[1] Anchorite, ankret or hermit.

promise to do no man harm. " Robert fell on his knees
with grete devocyon and repentaunce of his synnes, saynge,
Holy Fader, nay, as longe as I lyve I promyse god and his
blessyd mother I wyll never hurte crysten creature."

Then the Pope heard his confession—which was of such
an extraordinary nature, that he shrank from the responsi-

Robert.

bility of giving him absolution ; but told him he must go
to his own confessor, a hermit who lived three miles from
the city, tell him who had sent him, and he would hear
the confession and assoil him. So the next morning
Robert paid the hermit a visit. He was welcomed by the
holy man, who listened to his confession ; but he, like the

Pope, thought it so extraordinary, that he preferred to let the night go over before he pronounced absolution and set him his penance.

So all night Robert lay in the little chapel, and the hermit prayed fervently for guidance as to this singular case, until at last he fell asleep. In his slumber, an angel appeared unto him, and told him that it was God's command that if Robert would be shriven of his sins, he must counterfeit the ways and manners of a fool, and pretend to be dumb, and that he must eat no kind of meat but what he could take from the dogs; and this life he must lead until God should show him that his sin was forgiven. At daybreak the hermit called Robert to him, and told him of the penance which had been imposed upon him by the Divine will; and Robert accepted it thankfully, if, by so doing, he could only get rid of the intolerable load of his sins: and, after taking leave of the hermit, he went his way.

And as he entered Rome, he began to leap and run about like a lunatic, so that the children ran after him, and pelted him with mud and filth, and the people, at their windows, mocked and jeered at him. At length he came to the Emperor's Court, and, finding the gate open, went boldly into the hall, where he began curvetting and prancing about in such a manner, as to attract the emperor's attention, who, thinking it a pity that so good-looking a young man should be out of his mind, ordered one of his servants to give him some meat ; but he would have none of it. In those days the hounds were always participants of their master's meals in hall, and the emperor having thrown a bone to one of his dogs, Robert immediately seized it ; but, as the dog would not let go, he sat down and gnawed at one end of the bone, whilst the dog gnawed the other.

This conduct filled the emperor and his guests with astonishment, and seeing the poor witless fellow was really hungry, they cast more bones to the dogs, so that they might have the amusement afforded by the struggle between man and beast. Where the dogs quenched their thirst, so did he ; and when, at night, one went to lie down under the stairs, there he followed and lay beside it ; and when, by the emperor's orders, a bed was offered him, he refused it, and lay upon the damp earth. And thus he lived for seven years, eating, drinking, and sleeping with the dogs.

Now the emperor had a fair daughter, who was dumb, with whom the Seneschal was in love, and, because the emperor refused him her hand, he gathered an army of Saracens and laid siege to Rome ; and, although the emperor had the greatest number of men, yet would the Seneschal have got the advantage had it not been for Robert. For whilst the forces were engaged, he was by a fountain in a garden, when he heard " a voyce oute of Heven sente frome our Lorde, saynge in this manner :

Robert, god commandeth you by me that ye incontynent arme you with this harneys, and lyght upon this horse that god hath sente you, and ride in all the hast possyble and rescue th' emperour and his people." There was no mistaking this Divine command—there were the horse and armour. So Robert did as he was bid, and was soon riding to the battle-field, but he had been watched with wonder by the dumb princess. The day ended in a victory for the emperor, for " whan Robert was come in to ye hoost he put hym in the moost prese[1] of the turkes, and faughte and layde on eche syde on these cursed houndes. There a man myght have sene arms, legges, hedes, tomble on the grounde ; he smote to ye grounde both horse and man that never rose after ; it was a worlde to see ye murdre that Robert dyde amonge ye dampned dogges the sarasyns."

The victory assured, Robert returned to his fountain, unarmed, and both arms and horse vanished, to the extreme astonishment of the princess, who was a spectator of the strange scene. At night there was feasting, and the poor fool played his pranks as usual in the hall ; but it was noticed that he had a cut on his face, which was attributed to some of the servants having ill-used him. Of course the talk was chiefly on the champion who had so marvellously befriended them, and who had so mysteriously disappeared; and at each mention of his name the dumb princess pointed to Robert, and made signs that he it was who had so

[1] Thickest of the fight.

helped them : but this was so inconceivable that the emperor got angry at the suggestion, and the princess wisely left off.

The Seneschal, not content with his defeat, gathered another army, but was overthrown again by Robert's potent aid. He again disappeared, observed of none save the princess. Yet a third time the Seneschal besieged Rome, this time with a greater force than ever. Robert's prowess once more gained them the victory; but it happened that certain of the emperor's knights were determined to penetrate the mystery of the miraculous champion on the white horse, and waylaid him on his return. As he refused to answer their interrogations, and set spurs to his horse, one of the knights better mounted than his fellows followed in pursuit, and, wishing to kill the white horse in order to secure the strange knight, he missed the horse with his spear, but ran it into Robert's thigh, where it broke off ; and the white horse and its rider duly reached the fountain in the garden, where the steed, as usual, disappeared.

Robert drew out the spear-head, and hid it among the stones by the fountain, bathed his wound, and dressed it with grease and moss—watched all the time by the princess, who saw that he was comely and fair to look upon, and began to love him. Robert went into hall as usual, limping as little as he could, but enduring agonies of pain. By and by the knight who had wounded him returned, told his story, and expressed his sorrow that he should have hurt so worthy a knight ; and the emperor, by the advice of his nobles, issued a proclamation that, if the knight on a white horse would come to court, and bring with him the spear-head with which he was wounded, he would give him his daughter in marriage, and half his kingdom.

The Seneschal heard of this proclamation, and a bright thought struck him that he would drive a spear into his thigh, and go and claim the reward. This he did, and, although the knight was present who had wounded Robert, and knew it was not his spear-head, yet he spoke not, for fear that the Seneschal should kill him. So the Seneschal was awarded the prize. As for the lady, when she heard her fate, " she raylled and raged as thoughe she hadde ben wood and madde, she tare her here from her heed, and all to tare her clothes, but it myght nothynge avayle her, for she was constrayned and must be arayed like a bryde and an Emperour's doughter that shold be maryed."

Weeping and struggling, she was led to the altar, but hardly had the service commenced, when her fettered tongue was loosed, and she began to tell what she had seen ; when the Seneschal, perceiving that his chance was for ever gone, mounted his horse and fled away. She not only told of Robert and the white horse, but sent for the spear-head, which was found exactly to fit the shaft. Now were lords sent to fetch Robert, " whome they founde lyenge amonge dogges ; they folowed hym and dyd hym reverence, but Robert answered them not." The hermit

22

who had been warned by a dream, and had come to see to the rehabilitation of Robert, recognized him, and told him that God had forgiven all his sins, and in future he should be called no longer Robert the Devil, but Robert the servant of God. Then Robert fell upon his knees, and gave laud and thanks to God for his mercies and forgiveness. The emperor would have given him his daughter in marriage, but this the hermit would not suffer.

But, when Robert had gone but a little way from Rome, God commanded him to return and marry the princess ; which he did, and, after the usual prolonged festivities, he led his bride to Rouen. Here he found his father dead, and, consequently, that he was Duke of Normandy. Soon afterwards, he received a message from the Emperor of Rome, saying he was again besieged by the Seneschal, and begging his help. He at once went to his assistance, but found the emperor had been killed by the Seneschal. He had the satisfaction of cleaving the latter's head to the teeth, thus ending his vile life. This done, he returned to Rouen, and we learn that " Robert lyved long in vertue and honoure with that noble ladye his wyfe, and he was beloved and dradde [1] of hyghe and lowe degre, for he dyde ryght and justyce, as well over the ryche as over the poore kepynge his lande in rest and in prase."

---

[1] Feared.

Here beginneth a me

rye Jest of a man that was called Howleglas, and of many meruaylous thynges and
Jestes that he dyd in his lyfe, in East-
land and in many other places.

Ibowleglas.

HOWLEGLAS is one of the oldest jest-books in the English language, and it comes from a German source, the popular Eulenspiegel—literally *Owl* and *Glass*, as represented in the next illustration, which is taken from an early printed French edition. Eulenspiegel was in existence long before the merry tales of Skelton, or Scoggin's Jests, and its stories, like theirs, are not all reproducible for modern readers. The book from which I have taken this "Merye Jest" is very rare, there being but three copies known, two of which (unfortunately both imperfect) are in the British Museum, and the other is in the Bodleian Library. This latter was reproduced and privately printed by Frederic Ouvry, Esq., F.S.A., in 1867. The copies in the British Museum were "❡ Imprynted at London in Tamestrete at the Vintre on the Craned wharfe by Wyllyam Copland," and, in the catalogue, are approximately dated 1528 and 1530; but this is probably erroneous, being antedated, most likely, by some five and twenty or thirty years.

However, this does not detract from its rarity, and I now present it to my readers as a popular book of light reading and humour, coeval with the Romances.

"Yn the lande of Sassen, in the vyllage of Ruelnige, there dwelleth a man that was named Nicholas Howleglas, that had a wife named Mypeke, that lay a child bed in the same vyllage : and that chylde was brought into a taverne where the father was with his gosseppes, and made good cheret.

Whan the mydwife had wel dronke, she took ye childe to bere it home, and in the wai was a little bridg over a muddy water. And as the mydwife would have gone over the lytel brydge, she fel into the mudde with the chylde, for she had a lytel dronk to much wyne, for had not helpe come quickly, they had both been drowned in ye mudde. And whan she came home with the childe, they made a kettle of warm water to be made redi, and there they washed ye child clen of the mudde. And thus was Howleglas thre tyms in one dai cristened, once at ye churche, once in the mudde, and once in ye warm water."

Of course, with such a start in life, he could not but turn out something uncommon, and during his childhood he was preternaturally sharp ; but he was more than that—he was elvishly mischievous, so that he became notorious for his pranks, and, for amusement, he was very fond of dancing on the tight-rope. There is a tale told of him of

" Howe Howleglas fell from the rope into the water, whereof the people had good sporte.

"Upon a tyme Howleglas played upon ye corde that was set over the water, where he made good sport, but at the last there was one that cut the rope, so fell he into the water, and was all to wette, and he came out as well as he might, for ye lytle spyte he thought to quyte them agayn. And said to them, come agayne to morowe, and I will doo many more wonders upon the rope. And ye next dai after

came Howleglas and daunced upon the corde, and than he
sayde to the yonge folke, ye shall see what news I can doo.
Gyve me every body your ryghte shoe upon the rope end.
So they dyd, and the olde men also. And whan he hadde
daunced a whyle, he caste them their shoen upon a hepe,
and bad them take their shoen eche of them agayne.
Than ran they after their shoen, and for haste one tumbled
over the other, and than they began to ly together by the
eares, and smyte with their fystes so hard that they fell
both to the yearth. One said weping, this is my shoe, and
the other laughed and cryd that is my shoe. And thus, for
their shoen, they laye together by the eares. Than began
Howleglas to laughe, crying seeke your shoen. Yesterday
ye bathed me, and he lept from the corde, and went his
way to his mother, and durst not come out again in the
space of a moneth. And so he taried with his mother,
whereof his mother was glad, but she knew not the cause
why he dyd with her, nor what he had done."

He continued to grow up in this harum-scarum, ne'er-
do-well sort of fashion, until we hear

"How Howleglas was hired of a priest.

"As Howleglas ran out of yᵉ castel he came to a village
that was called Buddest, in the land of Brounswike. And
then came a priest to Howleglas, and hyred hym, but he
knew him not. The priest sayd to hym, that he should
have good dayes and eate and drinke the same meate that

he himselfe and his woman dyd, and al that should be
done with half the labour ; and than sayd Howleglas that
thereafter would he do his diligence. Then dressed the
priestes woman t(w)o chikins, and she bad Howlegas turne
(the spit), and so he dyd, and he loked up and saw that she
had but one iye, that whan the chikyns were (cooked)
enough, then he brake one of the chikins from the spit and
eate it without any bread, and when it was dener tyme,
came the woman unto ye kechin, where Howleglas turned,
and thought to take up the chikyns ; and whan she was
come, she founde no more there but one chikyn. Than
sayde she to Howleglas, where is the other chikyn : there
were two chykins ? Than answered he to her, lift up your
iye, and than shal you see the other chiken. Than was
the woman therewith angry, and knew well that Howleglas
mocked her, and than she ran to the priest and told him
howe she had dressed ii chykins, and whan she came to
take them up shee found but one, and than he mocked me
because I had but one iye : than went the priest to Howleglas and said, whi mocke ye my woman ; there was ii
chikyns. Than answerd Howleglas and said that was
truth. I have said to the woman that she should open her
eyen, and she should se well where that other chekyn was
become. Than laughed the priest and sayd she cannot se,
she hath but one iye : than sayd Howleglas to the priest,
the one chykin have I eaten, for ye sayd that I shold eate
and drinke as well as you and your woman, and the one

I eate for you, and the other I eate for your woman, for I was afrayde that you should have synned, for the promise that ye promysed me, and therefore I made mesure.

"Than sayd the priest, I care not for the chikens, but I wold have you please my woman, and do after her.   Then sayd Howleglas, I do your commaundement ; and that ye woman bad him do, he did but halfe, for she bad him fetch a boket of water, and he went and brought it but halfe full of water, and whan he shold brynge two logges, he brought but one, and when he should geve the beastes two botels of hay, he gave them but one, and when he should fetch a pot full of bere, he brought it halfe full, and so did he of many other things mo.[1]   Than complayned she to the priest of Howleglas again.   Than sayd ye priest, I bad that you should do as she bad you ; and Howleglas answered, I have done as ye bad me, for ye said to me that I should do al thing with halfe laboure.   And your woman would fayne se with both iyes ; but she seeth but with one iye, and so do I half ye labour.   And than the priest laughed : and than said ye woman, wyl you have this ungracious knave ani longer, then will I tarry no lenger with you, but depart.

"Than gave the priest Howleglas leve to depart for his woman's sake; but whan the paryshe clerke was dead of ye village, than sent the priest for Howleglas, and holpe hyme so muche that he was made the paryshe clerke."

[1] More.

How he behaved himself in his new position we shall see
by the following.

"And than in the meane season while Howleglas was
paryshe clarke, at Easter they should play the resurrection
of our Lord; and for because that the men wer not learned,
nor could not read, yᵉ priest took his leman,¹ and put her
in the grave for an aungell, and this seeing, Howleglas toke
to hym ii of the symplest persons that were in the towne,
that plaied the iii maries, and the parson plaied Christe,
with a baner in his hand ; than saide Howleglas to the
symple persons, whan the aungel asketh you whome you
seke, you may saye, the parsones leman with one iye.
Than it fortuned that the tyme was come that thei must
playe, and the angell asked them whom they sought, and
then said they as Howleglas had shewed and lerned them
afore ; and than answered they, we seke the priest's leman
with one iye, and than the priest might heare that he was
mocked.

"And whan the priestes leman herd that, she arose out of
the grave and would have smyten, with her fist, Howleglas
upon the cheke, but she missed him, and smote one of the
simple persons that played one of the thre maries, and he
gave her another, and than toke she him by the heare, and
that seing his wyfe, came running hastely to smite the
priest's leman; and then the priest seeing this, caste downe
hys baner, and went to helpe his woman, so that the one

¹ Love.

gave the other sore strokes, and made greate noyse in the churche.   And than Howleglas seyng them lyinge together by the eares in the bodi of the church, went his way out of the village, and came no more there."

" How Howleglas made hole al the sicke folke that were in the Hospitall, where the spere of our Lorde is.

" Upon a tyme Howleglas came to Northeborough, and he set upon the churche dores and upon ye Guyld hal, and every place that all the people in that towne myght knowe that he was a great maister of Phisicke : that al sicke he could make hol. And than the maister of the spytle house, where the spere of our lord is, had mani sicke folkes in his house. Than went the maister of the hospytall to Howleglas, and asked hym, yf he could helpe sicke men, or lame men, and make them hole ; and he would reward him after his owne pleasure.

" Then answered Howleglas to the maister of the hospitall, wyl ye geve me .r.r. golde gyledens,[1] and I shal recover and make them hole of all the sickness and deases,[2] and will have no money tyll all the sicke persons be delivered out of the hospital. These wordes pleased the maister of the hospitall veri wel. And he gave hym some money in his hande.

" Upon ye morowe after came Howleglas to the hospital with ii men after hym, and than he asked ye sicke folke,

---

[1] Guldens.   [2] Diseases.

one after the other, what desease they had ; and whan he
hadde asked them all, than he made them swere upon a
booke that they should kepe his counsail whatsoever he
said to them. They answered that they would : than saide
Howleglas to them, I have undertaken to make you all
hole, whiche is unpossible, but I must nedes bren one of
you all to pouder : and then must I take the powder of
him, and geve all ye others to drinke thereof, with other
medicines that I shall minister therto. And he that is the
last, whan I shal cal you out of the hospitall, and he
cannot go, shal be he that shal be brenned. For on
wednesday next coming, than shall I come before the
maister of the hospitall, and than shall I call, and he that
slepeth longest shall pay for al.

"Than prepared every one of ye sicke folke their crutches,
and gear, that they wold not be the laste. And whan
Howleglas was come to the maisters of ye hospitall, than
called he them, and than they ran out of the hospitall, and
some of them had not bene out of their bed in .r. yere
before. Than whan the sicke folke were out of the hospital, then asked he his money, and than the maister gave
it him, and than he departed.

"And within iii daies after came again the poore men to
the hospital, and complained of their sicknes, and than the
maister of the hospital said to them, how cometh this to
passe. I gave ye maister of phisik a great summe of
money to make you hole. Than answered the poore folke,

he hath deceyved you and us bothe, for foure dayes past he came to every one of us, and sayd to us that he should come on Wednisday next coming, and heale us, but he sayd he must nedes first bren one of us, and sayd that should be he that, when he shold cal, should be the last out of hys bed, and the pouder of hym shold they drinke, and be made hole therwith. Than knewe the maister of the hospitall that he was deceyved and begyled, and than toke he the poor folke into the hospitall, and put every one in their bedde, as they were before, but he dyd all agaynst his wyll."

Fraud and subtlety were the breath of his nostrils, and he lived shiftily and by his wits, as the annexed example will show.

"How Howleglas tooke upon him to be a painter.[1]

"Than it fortuned that Howleglas myght no longer tary in the land of Sassen for hys knavishenesse : than departed he into the land of Hessen to Marchborough to the earle, and he asked Howleglas what occapacion he was of ? Then answered Howleglas, worshipfull lord I am a painter, my cunning doth excell al other, for in no land is not so cunning as I. Then answered y[e] erle, have you here any ensample of your work ? Then answered Howleglas to the erle, yes my lord. Then had he be(en) in Flaunders, and brought with him divers ymages that pleased the

---

[1] This story is wanting in both the British Museum copies, and I have therefore taken it from Mr. Ouvry's reprint.

erle wonderfull well. Then sayd the earle to Howleglas, Master, what shal I geve to you to take upon you to paint upon the wal in my hal, al the lordes and knightes of my progeny, from the fyrst unto ye last in ye goodlyest and fayrest manner that ye can, with al the erles of Hessen and their ladies with them, and how our forfathers were married to ladies of straunge lands. And al this must you cast that it may be upon the walls of my hall.

" Then answered Howleglas to the earle, worshipfull lorde, if it please you that you wyll have all thys that you have rehersed to me to be painted so costli and rychly as you speake of, then would it cost, onely the colours that should (be)long thereto, above iii.c. golde geldens. Then answered the earle to Howleglas and sayd make yt well, and in the best maner, that you and we twaine shal agree after the beste maner. And also I shall doo you a greater pleasure than all that come thereto. And then toke Howleglas the woorke upon hym, but he sayd to the lorde, that he must nedes have an .c. gildens, in earnest to bi the colours that belonged thereto, and for his men's wages. And then bad the earle the rent maister geve to Howleglas an .c. geldens, and so he did.

" Then went Howleglas and gat him thre felowes, and then came he again to the earle and asked him a bone before he began to worke ; and ye erle graunted him, and then he did aske of the earle, that there should no person be so hardy to come into the hall to trouble him and his

workemen, without they aske hym lycence. And the
erle granted his desire : and than went Howleglas into the
hal with his servauntes, and whan he and they were in the
hall, Howleglas set a paire of tables ¹ before them, and he
bad them play, but he made them before to sweare that
they shoulde not bewraye him ; and the felowes had good
pastime, wherewyth they were wel content, and glad that
they might have meat, drinke, and cloth, and doo no other
thinge, but play and passe the time in that maner. And
Howleglas did no other thinge, but hang a white cloth
before yᵉ wall. That done, he came and plaied with hys
servauntes. In the meane time longed the earle greatly to
see his worke, if it was so goodly as the copy was, and to
se if the coloures were good, and so he departed and came
to Howleglas and said : Good maister painter, I pray you
let me go with you to se your worke. Then said Howleglas to the lord, worshipfull lord, before that you see mi
worke, I must shew to you one thinge. He, the which is
not borne in wedlocke, may not see my painting. Then
sayd the erle, that wer a merveylous thinge.

  " And then went he with Howleglas into the hall, and
there had he hanged up a white cloth (over) that he should
have painted. And he had in his hande a whit rod, and
he did awaye (with) the cloth that hanged upon yᵉ wal,
and pointed upon the wall with his whit rode, and shewed
the erle that that was the first lord of yᵉ land and erle of

¹ For draughts or backgammon.

Hessen. And this is yᵉ erle of Rome, he had a wife that they called Iustine, the Duke's doughter of Benem. And after that he was made Emperour. And of yᵉ daughter of him came Adulphus. And of Adulphus came William the swarte.[1] And this William had one Lewis, so forthe to your noble grace. And I know well that there is no parson livinge that can deprove my workes, so cureously have I made, and with faire colours ; but the Lord saw no worke, but yᵉ plain wal.

"Then thought he in his minde, am I a bastard—I see nothing but the whit wal. And for because that he would not be knowen for a bastard, he said to Howleglas, maister, your woorke pleaseth me merveylously well, but my understandinge is very small therein. And with that he went out of the hall, and came to his wife, and she asked him how that worke did please him ? he said I have shrewed[2] trust in him. Than said the erle, I like it well, shall it please you to looke theron, and she graunted. And then she desyred Howleglas that she might see his worke, and he graunted her, and then sayd unto her secretly, as he had sayd before to her lorde, and showed her the lordes upon the wal with the white rod in his hande ; as he did to the lord, and there stode one folishe gentilwoman with the lady, and she said, that she saw no painting on the wall, and the other spake not one worde. And then thought Howleglas, wyl this foole tel truthe : then must I

---

[1] Swarthy, or dark.   [2] Sure faith.

23

needes depart. Then hanged he up the white cloth, and so departed the lady.

" And when she was come to her lord, he asked her how she lyketh the worke she sayd ; how that it liketh me, it liketh not my folish gentlewoman, and she sayd that some of her gentle women say that it was but deceyte, and so thought the lord ; then sayde the lord to Howleglas, that he should make redy his worke that he and his lords might se it tomorow, that he might know which of them were borne in wedlocke and which were not, for he that is not borne in wedlocke, al his land is forfet to me. Then answered Howleglas, I wyll do it with a good wyl. Then went he to the rent maister, and received of him a .c. gold gildens.

" And when he had received the mony, he sayde to his servaunts, Now must we all departe, and gave them mony, of the which they were contente, and so departed. Then, on the morow came the earle with his lordes into the hall, and they asked wher the maister painter was, and his company, for he sayd he would see the worke. Then turned he up the cloth, and asked them if they sawe any worke, and they sayde nay. Then sayd the erle, we be deceived. He sayd we have sore longed to se Howleglas, and nowe he hath begyled us, but it maketh no great mater for the mony. But let us banishe him from our land for a begiler of people, and so they did. And so departed the earle with hys lordes."

" How Howleglas won a pece of clothe of a man
of the countrey.

"Howleglas would ever fare wel, and make good chere,
but he woulde not worke. Then on a time came he to
Olsem, to a goodly company of men of that countrey.
And as he walked, he espyed one man alone with a grene
cloth on hys arme ; then ymagyned he in his minde, how
that he might get yᵉ clothe. So he came to him, and he
asked him wher he was dwellyng. And then the husbandman tolde him ; and than departed Howleglas from him
and continentli[1] he met with a Shottish[2] priest, and
another knave, and he sayd to them, I desyre you to helpe
me, and I shall geve you for your labour, and they sayd
they wold. Than said Howleglas, whan I call you to
recorde to know what colour yonder cloth is ye shall say
blewe. I wil go before, and come [ye] after. Than went
he to the husbandman, and he asked him how he sold his
blewe cloth. Than sayde the husbandman, that it was grene
and not blewe. I hold .ɣɣ. gildens against thy cloth, that
it is blewe : than saide the husbandman I holde you. It is
done sayde Howleglas, and the first man that comes hereby,
shall be the judge thereto : agreed, sayd the husbandman.

" Than made Howleglas a sygne to the men, that he had
hired, and they came. Than sayde the husbandman, we
two strive what colour this cloth is, I pray you breke our
stryfe. Than the felow saide it is fayre blew cloth ; than

---

[1] Soon.   [2] Scotch.

said ye husbandman, man, ye be too false for me to medle
with, for it is made betwyxt you two to deceyve me.   Than
sayde Howleglas, cause that ye saye we be agree, let hym
go ; here cometh a priest, wil ye be contented what he
sayeth : and the man of the countre sayde yes.   Than
came the priest by : than sayd Howleglas, I praye you to
tel us what colour this cloth is ?   The priest sayd, ye se
wel ynough, what nede you to aske me.   The husbandman
sayd, I know the colour of the cloth wel ynough, but these
two men say it is an other colour, and therefore we stryve.
Than sayde the priest, what have I to do with your
stryving ?   Than sayde the husbandman, I pray you syr,
departe us of our stryving.   Than sayde the priest, I can
se no other, but that it is a fayre blewe.   And than sayd
the husbandman, and ye were not a priest, in fayth ye did
lye, for ye be thre false men : but sythen ye be a priest I
must beleve you.   And then gave he Howleglas the cloth,
and wente his waye.   Than did Howleglas with his ii
felowes clothe themselves with the husbandman's cloth
againste the wynter.   But the good poore man prayed to
God many a tyme and ofte, that the devill might take
them al thre, for the poore man was then worse all the
dayes of hys lyfe after that great losse."

"Howe Howleglas gave .x. gyldens to .xii. poore
men for christes love.

"On a time came Howleglas to Hanover, where he did

many vertuous thinges. On a time rode Howleglas
without the towne, and as he rode he met with .ʀíí. blinde
men to whom he saide, whether wil ye go? The blinde
men hering that he was on horseback they put off their
cappes, for they wende [1] that he had beare a great gentleman, and saide, we have bene at a doole [2] of a ryche man,
that died yesterdai in the town. Than sayd Howleglas, I
take gret thought for you, how you shall do this winter,
for methink you shall frese to death, before the winter be
done. And than he sayde, holde, here is .ʀʀ. gildens, and
returne agayne all you to the place where that I was
lodged, and he named his host, and he bad them make
good chere til winter were done.

"And than they thanked hym, for they thought that
he had geven them moni, but he did not. And then
departed they to the place whither he sent them, and
they thought that some of the company had the mony.
And whan they came to the Inne, they said to the
hostise that, by the way as they went, thei met with
a good man that gave them .ʀʀ. gildens for god's
sake, and he bad us come hither, and make good chere
therefore, for he sayd that he had bene lodged here, and
for his sake we shold have good chere. Whan the hoste
herde that they had mony, he toke them in, and made
them good chere.

"And whan that their .ʀʀ. gildens were spent, than said

---

[1] Weened, thought or imagined.   [2] Mourning.

the hoste to them. Nowe will ye reken, good brethren, for now the .ᴦᴦ. gildens be spent. The blynd men sayd, we be contented to pay you, and than spake one of the blinde men, and sayd, He that hath twenty gildens pay our hoste. And than said the one to the other, I have not the .ᴦᴦ. gyldens ; Nor I have not the twenty gyldens. And than some sate and clawed their head, and some clawed their arme. And than they knew that they were deceyved. Than thought the hoste in hys mynde, what shall I do with them ? Shall I let them go that they spend me no more mony ? Nay, not so. Than shut he the blind men in the stable, and brought to them hay and strawe.

And whan that Howleglas thought that al the mony was spent, than came he ryding in to the same Inne where the blynde men were, and he had chaunged hys clothyng that they should not knowe hym, and so entred into the Inne where the blynd men were, and he led his horse into the stable wher the pore men were. And (when) he had set up his horse, he came to his hoste, and asked his hoste wherfore he had kept the blynd men in the stable, so fast shut in. And he asked him what harme they had done to hym. Than sayd the hoste, I would that they were together in the water so that I had my costes payde me, and than he tolde him all the matter. And than sayde Howleglas. And you had a borowe,[1] would you lette them goo. And the hoste sayde yes, with a good wyll.

[1] If you had a surety.

Than sayde Howleglas, I wyll go see if I can finde any borowe for them.

"Then went he to the Curate of the churche and sayde, Maister parson, I have an hoste that this night was taken with the fende;[1] I desyre you for to helpe hym. The Curate saide, with a good wyll, but you must tary two or thre daies for it maye not be done in haste. Well, sayde Howleglas, that is well saide, but I will go fetche his wife, that she may here what you say. And ye priest said I shall tel to her the same that I told to you without fayle. And than went Howleglas home to his hoste, and he tolde hym that he had founde a borow, and that it was the parsone of the churche, and let your wyfe go with me, and she shall here him speke ye same that he hath sayde to me, and than was his hoste glad and he sende his wife with Howleglas, to the Curate. And whan they were come to the Curate, Howleglas said to him, Maister parsone here is the wyfe of the man, that I spake of to you, now tell her the same that you have said to me. And the curate sayd, with a good wil: than said he to the woman, tary a daye or two, and I shall helpe your husbande well. And than was the woman glad, and returned home agayne withe Howleglas, and whan she came home, she told her husband what the curate sayd, whereof the hoste was glad, and he went unto the stable, and let the blynde men lose and they went their way.

[1] Possessed by the devil.

" And than Howleglas reckned with his hoste, and so departed from thence ; and whan the thyrd day came, than went the woman to the priest, and she asked him twente gildens that the blynde men had spende. The curate asked her, hath your husbande that ye told to me ?[1] And the woman said no. Than said the Curate, that is the false devill that wold have the mony. Than saide she, what false devill menest thou ? Geve me mi moni for my costes. Than saide the curate to the woman, it was tolde me that your husbande was taken with ye false devyll ; brynge him hether, and I shall helpe hym thereof by the grace of god. Than sayd the woman to ye priest, suche begylers fynde I many. Now you should pay me for my costes ; you bring to me a back rekening, and you say my husband is taken with the devyll, and that you shall know shortly. And than she ran to her husbande, and tolde hym how the priest said to her.

" And whan the hoste heard those wordes, he was angry, and toke the spit with the rost that lai at the fyre, and ran to the priestes chambre. And whan the curate spyed him he was afrayde, and called the neighbours to help him, and he made a signe of the holy crosse before him, and he cryed for help to take that man that was so beset with the devil. Than sayd the hoste, thou priest pay me my mony, and the priest gave hym no aunswere. Than would the hoste have run thorow him with the hote spyt, but the

[1] He meant, is he possessed with the devil ?

neyghbours went betwene them and departed them, and
they helde the hoste stil with gret payne from maister
parsone. But as long as the hoste lived, he asked his
mony of the priest, for the costes of the blynde men, but
the priest aunswered to him that he ought him nought, and
nought he would pay him, but sayd, and you be taken with
a devyll, I shall helpe you therof. But never after, loved
one the other."

" How Howleglas scared his hoste with
a dead woulfe.

"In Ysetleven dwelled an Inneholder that was very
spyteful and mockying, and he praysed greatly his bold-
nesse. Upon a tyme, it befell in the winter season, when
there had been a great` snow, Howleglas came riding with
other thre merchauntes from Sasson to Ysetleven, and it
was very late or they came there; and when they were
come, they entred into the Inne that the man kept.
Than sayde their hoste angerly, wher have you ben so late,
it is no time now to take your Inne. Than they aunswered,
Be ye not angry, for we have been hounted with a woulfe
in the snow, we could not scape till nowe. Than the hoste
mocked them because they iiii were huntying of one
woulf, and said, if there came x woulfes to me in ye field,
I wold have slayne them everichone, and mocked y^e
marchauntes tyl they went to bed. And Howleglas sate

by the fyre and herde al together. Than should they go to bed.

"And it fortuned that Howleglas and the marchaunts should lye in one chambre. And when they ware in the chambre together, they toke counsayl together how they myght stop their hoste of his mocking. Then sayde Howleglas, our hoste is full of mocking; let me alone, I shall pay him well ynough that he shall not mocke us no more. Than promysed the marchauntes to Howleglas to pay all his costes, and geve hym more monye for his labour. Than sayde Howleglas, do your Journey and busynesse of your marchaundise, and whan ye have (done) it, come agayne and lodge at this Inne, and ye shal fynde me here, and then we shal make our host that he shal mocke no more. And than arose ye marchauntes in the morning, and payed hym for their costes, and Howleglas also. Than they took their horses and departed from thence. And whan they were paste a lytle, he cryed to the marchauntes, take hede that the woulfe byte you not, in mockage. They thanked their hoste because he gave them warning before.

"And, as they rode, Howleglas found a woulfe that was frozen to ye deth, and that he toke up, and put in a bagge, and layd it before him, and than they retourned agayne to Ysetleven, to that Inne wher they were lodged before. And he kept the woulf so close that no man knew therof. And whan the nyght was come and that they sat all at supper, than the hoste began to laugh at them, and he resoned against their hardines and against the woulfe. Than sayd they, so it fortuned at that time, you said that you would slay x woulfes, but first I wold se you kyl one. And then said yᵉ hoste that should I do alone. And thus they rested tyl they went to bedde.

" And Howleglas helde his peace, tyll that he and the marchauntes went above, all together in the chambre. And than sayd Howleglas to yᵉ marchauntes, Let me nowe begyn to worke, and wake you a lytle whyle. And than when the hoste and all his folke were a slepe, than wente he pryvely into the chambre, and he fetched the ded woulf that was styffe frosen, and dressed him with stickes, and put two chyldrens shoen in his mouth, and made him stand as though he had ben a live. And then left he yᵉ woulf standing in the hal, and he came againe into the chambre to yᵉ marchauntes, and when he was above, he and yᵉ marchauntes called their hoste. And their hoste asked them what they would have. Than aunswered they to him, that they would have some drynke, for they had so gret thyrste that they must nedes drynke. Let your mayd or man brynge us some, and we wyll paye for it tomorowe. Then waxed the hoste angrye and sayd, This is the Sasson's maner, for to drynke both daye and nyght. And than he called his mayd, and bad her that she should geve the merchauntes drinke.

" And than the mayde rose, and as she went to lyght a

candel, she saw the woulf with ii shoen in his mouth. Than she was afrayd, and ran to the gardeyn, for she thought that he had eaten both the chyldren ; than called they agayne. Than called the hoste his man, and bad him rise and bere the Sassons drynke. Than arose he, and lyghted a candle, for he wened that the mayde had slept still. Then looked he asyde and sawe the woulfe stande, (and) he was afrayd, and he thought that the woulfe had eaten the mayde, and let fal the candle, and ran into ye seller.

"Than called Howleglas and the marchauntes the third time, and prayed that he himself would bring them some drinke, for they sayde there came no bodye, or else geve them a candle and they wold drawe it themselfes. Than arose the hoste hymselfe, for he wend that his man and his mayde were fallen aslepe agayn, and than lyghted he a candle, and whan that he had done he loked asyde and spyed the woulfe : and he was so afrayde that he fel unto the ground, and than arose he and cryed to the marchauntes, and he prayed them for to come helpe him, for there was a woulf, that had eaten both his man and his mayde. And this herde the mayde in the gardeyn and the man in the seller, and come to helpe their maister, and the marchauntes also. And Howleglas laughed at this hardy man, that woulde have slayne ten woulfes, and he was made afraide of one deade woulfe. And whan theyr hoste saw that it was done in mockage, than was he ashamed, and he wyste not what to say. And than left he his bostying and jestying, and went to bed againe. And on the morow it was knowen through the towne, wherof the hoste was sore ashamed. And than in the morning arose the marchauntes and paied their costes, and Howleglas also, and rode their way. And than never after praysed the hoste his manhode."

As in life he was mischievous, so was he in his exit from this world ; *vide*

" How Howleglas made his testament.

" In the meane time waxed Howleglas sycker and sicker. Than he called for ye lordes to make his testamente. And whan they were come he gave his grodes in iii partes. One parte to his kynsfolke, another to the lordes of Molen, and the other to the parson of Molen whensover he died. And he asked to be buried in christen mans buriall, and to syng for hys soule, Placebo ^1 and Dirig, with masses and other good servyces, after the custome and usans.

" And than he shewed to them a great chest that was wel barred with yron, and foure keyes therto belonging, and he told unto them that in this chest was all his goods, and than he gave the cheste to them to kepe, that were right heavy for him. And than within a moneth after his death, than the foure should take the keyes therof, and deale all

---

^1 Two Antiphons in the Roman Catholic *Officium Defunctorum*. " Placebo Domino in regione vivorum " is sung at Vespers, and " Dirige Domine Deus meus, in conspectu tuo viam meam," at Matins.

the money for his soule. And within a whyle after he departed.

" And whan he was dead, they wound hym in a wynding shete, and after in a coffyn, and after on a bere. Than came the pryestes and feched hym to church, and sung for him Placebo and Dirig. And in the meane time came in a sow with her pygges, and went under the bere, for she had founde the taste of dead flesshe, and with her nose she cast down the bere, whereof the priestes and clerkes wer afrayde; and (when) they sawe that it was downe, than they ran so fast that eche fell on others necke, for the thought that he had bene rysen agayne, and so they lefte hym there. And than the systers of a nonnery took the corse, and brought to grave and buried it. And whan a moneth was past, than came the thre parties for to unlocke the cheste, and for to deale the money for his soule. And whan that they had opened the cheste, they founde no other but stones therin.

" Than they woundered therof, and the one looked on the other, and the parson wened that the lordes had had the money because they had the chest in kepinge. And the lordes wened that his frendes had opened the cheste and taken out the tresure, and put in stones the whyle that he was sycke, and so to have shut the cheste agayne. And his frendes wende that the curate had conveied the tresure whan that he confessed hym. And than in a gret anger they departed fro thence, for at the last they knew that it

was he that had done it for to mocke them. And after
that the lordes and the curate agreed together agayne, and
so to bury hym under the galowes. And so they dyd.
And, as they were delvinge of his grave, he stanke so sore
that they could not abide yᵉ ayre therof. And so they
covered hym wyth earth agayne, and lete hym lye styll,
and so they departed."

Glossary.

Adommage : hurt.
Advertyse : to acquaint.
Agayn : opposite, right before.
Almayne : Germany.
Almesses : alms.
Ancresse : a female hermit.
Apas : apace, quickly.
Appayre : damage.
Apyered : sticking out, projecting.
Arbelstre : an arbelast or cross-
   bow.
Auctowne : an Haqueton or quilted
   waistcoat, worn under the coat
   of mail.
Aunker : an anchorite or hermit.

Bable : talk.
Basse stone : window sill.
Bayne : hurt, injury.
Be : been.
Beforne : before.
Bende : to bow to circumstances.
Bewreke : avenge.
Blive : quickly.

Boone : bone.
Borowe : a burgh or town.
Borowe : a pledge, surety.
Borowe : to avail.
Bote : beat.
Braste : broke, burst.
Brere : underwood, briar.
Browded : embroidered.
Bruled : burnt.

Carfull : full of care.
Chaffed : angry, chafed.
Chyk : cheek.
Cleve : to open or rend asunder.
Clockarde : probably hand bells.
Clypping, or cleping : embracing.
Comite : county, district.
Conned : knew.
Continentli or incontinent : soon.

Damyse : damson.
Dede : caused.
Devoure : devoir or duty.
Dey : die.

Did on : put on.
Digne : worthy.
Do : to cause.
Dolaunt : sorrowful.
Doleur : grief.
Doo : done.
Doole : mourning.
Doon : caused.
Dormound : a dromond or armed vessel.
Doughtye : brave.
Dowcemere : a dulcimer.
Down-tere : to make long gashes.
Dradde : fear.
Dyghte : clad.
Dynt : stroke.

Echone : each, or every one.
Eerys : ears.
Erre : erst, before.
Eyen : eyes.
Eyled : ailed.

Fane : a weather-cock.
Fayne : glad.
Faytte : fact.
Fe or fee : property.
Flaugh : flew.
Fode : food.
Fonde : a token of affection, kindness.
For : sometimes used instead of from.
Foyson : a company, troop.
Fro : from.

Gent : gentle or soft.
Gentry : birth and breeding.

Getron : a musical instrument ; a gittern or zithern.
Glede : a red-hot coal.
Glytte : to slide.
Grome : a man.
Gyledens : guldens.   Flemish gold coins.
Gynnes : fastenings.

Hallowes : saints.
Happe : luck.
Harde : hardy, bold.
Heded : beheaded.
Hende : gentle, polite.
Hente : hold, clasped.
Hette : hit.
Herborow : to reside.
Hight : called.
Hole : whole.

Jurney : a day's work.

Kene : earnest, bold.
Kerle : ceorl or churl, a labourer.
Kerved : carved.
Kest : cast.
Kette : cut.
Knave : a man servant.

Lavorocke : a lark.
Lawe : hung.
Layne : delay.
Leasynge : lying.
Leeven : believe.
Lened : behindhand.
Lemman or leman : a lover.
Lente : to remain.
Lepe : to spring.

Lese : to lose.
Lese : lies.
Lore : lost.
Lough : laugh.
Lowe : a bright fire.
Lynee : lineage, family, or race.

Malison : a curse.
Manded : warned or bidden.
Maser tree : a hard-wood tree.
Mavis : the singing thrush.
Mawmetry : idolatry, from *mammet*
   —an idol, puppet, or doll.
Maye : a maid.
Mede or meede : reward.
Messe : missing.
Meyne : servants, followers.
Misculyne : a mixed metal.
Mo or mowe : more.
Mued : changed, transformed.
Musarde : a dreamer.

Naked : unarmed.
Ne : nor.
Noie : annoy, hurt, injure.
Nolde : would not.
Nuthake : the nuthatch.

On hye : loudly.
On live : alive.
Osyll : the ousel or blackbird.
Ottroye : give, utter.
Owche : a brooch.
Owe : ought.

Palfrener : a groom.
Pallade : a rich kind of cloth.
Parements : furniture.

Passed : surpassed.
Pautenere : a purse or pocket.
Pease : appease, quiet.
Pesaunt : heavy.
Penseful : pensive, full of thought.
Perde : *par Dieu*, by God.
Perfay : *par foi*, i' faith.
Playned : played with.
Popinjay : a parrot.
Price or Pryce : a prize.
Purfled : trimmed or edged.
Pyany : peony.

Rayed : dressed, arrayed.
Reck : to care about.
Record : a kind of flageolet.
Rede : to counsel, advise.
Relessed : relieved.
Rewfull : rueful.
Ribible : a kind of fiddle.
Roche : a rock.
Rood : a cross, crucifix.
Rote : a sort of cymbal.
Ruddocke : a robin.
Ruth : compassion, pity.

Salewed : saluted.
Sayne : say.
Seckerly : securely, surely.
Semblable : similar.
Semblaunt : resemblance, image.
Sered : enbalmed.
Shene : shining.
Shever : a slice.
Shrewed : sure.
Sith : since.
Slo or sle : to kill.
Sometime : formerly.

Sowned : swooned, fainted.
Sperhauk : a sparrow-hawk.
Spert : sudden.
Stercke : stark, stiff.
Sterte or start : leap down, alight.
Stonde : hurriedly.
Stounde : a little while.
Stounds : pains.
Sue : to follow, pursue.
Surrie : Syria.
Swarte : swarthy or dark.
Syde : aside.

Tables : draught or backgammon
    boards.
The : they.
Tho : then.
Thrustle : a thrush.
To : sometimes used instead of as.
To fore : towards.
Tonne : a barrel or large cask.
Toth : a tooth.
Tre : wood.
Tyll : thereof.
Tyres : attire, dress.

Uneathes : unfit, unwieldy.

Vavasour : a vassal.
Voyded : emptied.
Vylayne : villein, a labourer.

Waloping : galoping.
Wate : to lie in wait.
Welde : govern.
Wened : ween or fancy.
Wete : to know.
Whom : home.
Witted : twitted.
Wone : plenty, quantity.
Woode or wode : mad.
Woodwele : a woodpecker.
Worthied : was worth.
Wyght : active.
Wytte or wit : to know.

Ye : yea, yes.
Yede or yode : went.
Ywis : I think.

UNWIN BROTHERS, THE GRESHAM PRESS, CHILWORTH AND LONDON.

Lightning Source UK Ltd.
Milton Keynes UK
UKOW032020070213

205991UK00008B/249/P